P9-DXE-285

6 95 AB / 3

High on Foggy Bottom

Books by Charles Frankel

HIGH ON FOGGY BOTTOM

EDUCATION AND THE BARRICADES

THE NEGLECTED ASPECT OF FOREIGN AFFAIRS

THE LOVE OF ANXIETY AND OTHER ESSAYS

THE DEMOCRATIC PROSPECT

THE CASE FOR MODERN MAN

THE BEAR AND THE BEAVER

THE FAITH OF REASON

Books Edited by Charles Frankel

THE GOLDEN AGE OF AMERICAN PHILOSOPHY

ISSUES IN UNIVERSITY EDUCATION

THE USES OF PHILOSOPHY: AN IRWIN EDMAN READER

ROUSSEAU'S SOCIAL CONTRACT

High on

1817

Withdrawn by
Whitman College Library

Foggy Bottom

AN OUTSIDER'S INSIDE VIEW

OF THE GOVERNMENT

By *Charles Frankel*

HARPER & ROW, PUBLISHERS

NEW YORK, EVANSTON, AND LONDON

Portions of this book first appeared, in somewhat different form, in The Saturday Review, The Public Interest, *and* American Political Science Review.

The quotation on page 6 is from "Among School Children" taken from Collected Poems of W. B. Yeats. *Used by permission of M. B. Yeats and Macmillan & Co. Also with permission of The Macmillan Company from* Collected Poems *by W. B. Yeats. Copyright 1928 by The Macmillan Company, renewed 1956 by Georgie Yeats.*

HIGH ON FOGGY BOTTOM: AN OUTSIDER'S INSIDE VIEW OF THE GOVERN-MENT. *Copyright © 1968, 1969 by Charles Frankel. All rights reserved. Printed in the United States of America. No part of this book may be used or reproduced in any manner whatsoever without written permission except in the case of brief quotations embodied in critical articles and reviews. For information address Harper & Row, Publishers, Incorporated, 49 East 33rd Street, New York, N.Y. 10016. Published simultaneously in Canada by Fitzhenry & Whiteside Limited, Toronto.*

FIRST EDITION

LIBRARY OF CONGRESS CATALOG CARD NUMBER: 68-28196

To my colleagues in CU

155471

Contents

x   *Contents*

Foreword

The story told in this book is a true story, for all its elements of
implausibility. Between the summer of 1965 and the end of
1967, I served in the federal government as Assistant Secretary
of State for Educational and Cultural Affairs. When I entered
the government, the Johnson Administration was completing
two years of unparalleled legislative success. The war in Vietnam was a cloud on the horizon, but it was not quite thinkable
that the cloud would not blow away. It looked those days as
though the Johnson Administration could accomplish almost
anything it wanted, provided it stuck to its knitting.

I have no scandals to recount, and no morsels of hitherto un-
revealed information which will put all that happened during
the period in which I served in a new light. What I have to
report are merely the commonplaces of everyday life inside the
government of the United States. These are curiosities enough.

What is it like to live and work inside the government? What
does a man *do*—not in terms of an abstract job description, but
from moment to moment and day to day? What are the
pleasures, pains and dilemmas, the external frustrations and
inner satisfactions, of official life? What is the look and feel,

when you are inside it, of that elusive, rambling and inchoate thing which has come to be known, in a wistful and flattering phrase, as "the power structure"? My answers are one man's, and personal ones. They say as much about what went on in my own mind as about the external environment in which I lived. I hope they may help to bring the federal government, and the citizen's relation to it, back into the natural world again.

High on Foggy Bottom

1

The Taste of Power

"I'm Lillian Lovitz," said my secretary. "I come with the lease." Other things, as I discovered when I arrived in my new office, came with the lease too. The Lincoln Memorial was outside the window, and beyond it the bridge across the Potomac. I could see, across the river, the hillside in Arlington Cemetery with the white slash in it, which was the Kennedy grave. I sat down and looked through the drawers of my desk. I found a legacy of pennies, a shoebrush, a box of Kleenex and some Scotch tape. I felt something prick the calf of my leg, and then prick it again. I looked down and examined my swivel chair. A tack had come uncovered on the front of the chair. I covered it with the Scotch tape.

The walls of my office were paneled. Its floor was carpeted in green, wall-to-wall. It was identical, as I discovered when I subsequently visited my neighboring Assistant Secretaries, with their offices, which stretched down the great long corridor. The suite housing my immediate staff was identical to the square inch with the suites assigned to theirs. Whatever the relative importance of the Assistant Secretary of State for European Affairs, the Assistant Secretary for Economic Affairs, or the Assistant

Secretary for Cultural Affairs might be in the eyes of God or Congress, the General Services Administration, which approves the plans for government buildings, had made its statement: all Assistant Secretaries are equal.

Just above my office, on the seventh floor, were the offices of the Secretary of State and the Under Secretary. Seventh-floor rugs were blue; at the White House rugs were red. The offices of the Policy Planning Council of the Department were also on the seventh floor. It was obvious that policy was created at the top and dripped downward; it was obvious, at any event, to the General Services Administration.

Below me, on the fifth, fourth, third and second floors, with some overflow in other buildings, throbbed my Bureau, the Bureau of Educational and Cultural Affairs. I felt the throbbing. Messages from the Bureau percolated upstairs to me from the moment I entered my office. My staff assistant entered every two or three minutes with papers for me to sign. "CU" my Bureau was called—short for "culture." I was to hear those two letters spoken every day—I came to speak them myself—with the solemn affection with which other people say "Yale," or "Siwash" or "PS 478." On my first day, however, it seemed a little forced. Did the Bureau really feel to everyone in it like his old school?

But another message came through to me even more clearly. The State Department is a hierarchy. I went downstairs to visit the offices of my new colleagues in CU and discovered that the Office Directors, the bigger fish, had rugs in their offices, as I did, but their rugs weren't green, they were gray, and they weren't wall-to-wall. They had pictures of the President on their walls, but the pictures were in black and white. The picture in Assistant Secretaries' offices was in color. Everything, in this new territory into which I had moved, was carefully and visibly measured out. A difference in power that wasn't evident in the color of a rug was not a difference.

It was clear that I would not have to earn deference in this world. Frankness and confidence, however, might be harder to come by.

But CU wasn't waiting, like clay, to be molded to my heart's desire. When I plunged into the pile of letters on my desk, the truth hit me that I had fallen into something larger than myself. I finally knew what it meant to be in the grip of history. The letters had been written for me and were waiting for my signature. I offer my recollection of the letter on top of the pile. It has kept coming back to me early in the morning, at that hour before dawn breaks, when my resistance is low.

DEAR MR. JONES:
Your letter of the 21st is appreciated. The question that has been raised is under study. It is necessary that you be informed, however, that the results of this study are not expected for some time, and will themselves be subject to further review when they are received. Under the circumstances, it is felt that no answer can now be given to your inquiry. At such time as warranted by conditions, you will be informed.
Pending such time, it is requested that no further inquiry be directed to this office. Assurance is given of the existence of interest in inquiries such as yours emanating from the private sector.

The name at the bottom of the page—I recall the shock very distinctly—was my own.

I came to call the tone of voice that characterizes government correspondence "the public-passive voice." It has the standing, within the government, of a special grammatical mode, created specifically for the conduct of correspondence between a government and its citizens. Use of this voice gives to a letter the quality of coming from a world in which thoughts and emotions float around without belonging to anyone, in which decisions are always in process but are never made, and in which the buck, when it is passed, is passed unerringly into the void. A letter written in this voice conveys a proper sense of mystery. Reading between the lines, a citizen can learn the same lesson about government that Gertrude Stein is alleged to have learned about Oakland, California: when you get there, there is no there there.

After I read this letter, I made my way through some of the letters beneath it. I tried my hand at redrafting the letters. I put them in the first person singular, used active verbs, gave an unequivocal Yes to one inquiry, and said No to another. The letters came back to me in the evening, re-redrafted. I was having my first brush with the system.

The struggle was to go on for a couple of weeks. After a while, my colleagues in the Bureau developed a file of "cleared paragraphs." These were collected from letters that I had written myself, or that had got by me without my raising an objection. By the judicious shuffling of cleared paragraphs, a letter could be prepared for my signature that I could not, it was believed, send back. This system didn't work well at first because I am a severe critic of my own prose, and it created other problems as well. Letters constructed out of cleared paragraphs, forthright and unequivocal though they might be, often didn't answer the questions asked. But in the course of time the system smoothed itself out. This is the public-passive way of saying that I stopped fighting it so hard.

The merits of the public-passive voice are of course considerable. It permits the writer of a letter to glide away into a nameless nowhere; the opposition, in consequence, cannot be quite sure that it is opposing anyone or anything and becomes discouraged. There is animal cunning in this kind of prose. There are problems in government that can only be solved by being buried, and the public-passive voice is more than simply a technique for passing the buck. It is the technique of losing the damn thing so that it won't trouble people again.

My impression that first day was that I had suddenly fallen into a whirlpool. A Presidential assistant called to ask if I could immediately prepare the first draft of a speech for the President. A telephone call came from Tokyo, telling me that the *Hello, Dolly!* company which was on tour for the Department was in a state between mutiny and suicide because the Soviet Union had suddenly canceled its projected visit to Moscow. Members of the company were about to let the Soviet authorities have it in the newspapers, and, having worked up steam, they were probably going to let the State Department have it too. The Executive Director of the Bureau came in and put the budget for the next fiscal year in front of me; a Deputy Assistant Secretary told me that one of the best men in CU was about to transfer unless I could prevail on him to stay; a group came in to brief me on the status of negotiations with the Japanese; another group told me about the status of negotiations with the Soviet Union over the cultural agreement; a third group reviewed for me our negotiations with the Office of Education on the administration of programs in the United States for foreign teachers. The negotiation with the Office of Education seemed to be the most difficult.

And through it all, the slow, impassive background music of State Department routine swelled and faded: the door would open, and more letters and memoranda would be put before me to sign. By the end of the day, shadowy images were spinning by me of theater people who had never heard of rules, of bureaucrats who had never heard of anything but rules, and of the President, turning up to give a speech, and opening the text and finding only blank pages. The pauses in the day when I could regroup my thoughts came while I gave a ten-minute talk to a group of foreign visitors, and during a formal ceremony when I stood among the dignitaries accepting, on behalf of the United States, a statue from the Greek Ambassador.

In a sense, I had known that "power" might feel like this, just as I had known, before I ever had a drink, that whisky goes to the head. The taste of power, or whatever it was that

I tasted that first day, went to my head too, but not quite as I had been warned it would. I had come into the office with projects and plans. And I was caught in an irresistible movement of paper, meetings, ceremonies, crises, trivialities. There were uncleared paragraphs and cleared ones, and people waiting for me to tell them what my plans were, and people doing things that had nothing to do with my plans. I had moved into the middle of a flow of business that I hadn't started and wouldn't be able to stop. There were people in place to handle this flow, and established machinery in operation to help me deal with it. The entire system was at my disposal. In a word, I had power. And power had me.

> O body swayed to music, O brightening glance,
> How can we know the dancer from the dance?

What had brought this dancer to the dance?

2

Crossing the Divide:
Excerpts from a Log

July, 1965:

Chatting on the telephone with P.H., I told him that Helen and I were beginning to look for a house in rural New York where we could spend our time in between the academic years. A half-hour later he called back to say that I'd better start looking for a house in Georgetown. The chief of staff of the Foreign Relations Committee had just been in touch with him, asking questions about me.

So the rumors have some substance. A man who knows somebody who knows somebody told me just the other day that the position of Assistant Secretary of State for Cultural Affairs could be mine if I only let the word go out that I was interested. But I'm not sure that I am interested. I merely hope, after the study of American cultural policy that I've just completed, that somebody gets the job who wants to make some reforms. In any case, I should be surprised, in view of the report that I've written, if the job were offered to me. So I'm not giving it enough thought to know whether I'm interested.

✳

I received a call from the White House today, and somehow, to my surprise, I wasn't surprised. One of the President's assistants telephoned to ask if I'd be interested in becoming Assistant Secretary. He put it carefully: he wasn't asking if I'd take the job because he wasn't in a position to offer it to me; but *if* it were offered, what would I say? I said, in reply, that it would be nice to be asked—*if* I were asked—but that it was also nice to be living as I was. Besides, it was hard to compare a bird in the hand with a hypothetical bird in the bush.

The President's man was understanding, but asked if I'd at least come down to Washington to discuss the hypothesis. He told me that a number of people on the White House staff had read my report with interest and approval. And the most immediate point of his call was to say that Senator Fulbright was eager to see me. I agreed to go down to Washington and talk it over.

✳

I spent the day in Washington. The key figure in the picture is Senator Fulbright. The President has indicated to the Senator that if he and the individuals he has designated from the White House staff can get together on a man, the President will name that man. The Senator and these individuals hope I will let them put my name before the President. Supervision of the Fulbright exchange program is, of course, one of the responsibilities of the man who holds this job, but that is only one of the reasons—a minor one, I think—for the Senator's active interest in who is to be chosen. For much more general reasons, this is the post in the State Department which Senator Fulbright probably identifies most closely with his kind of approach to foreign affairs. And although nobody has said so in so many words, I get the scent that the Senator is troubled about aspects of the Administration's foreign policy, and that this appointment is one way in which the President is seeking to reassure him.

I talked with Senator Fulbright in his office. He had been doing his reading, he knew my views, and he urged me, most seriously, to accept the assignment. Yet I don't recall anybody's ever asking me to do a job in quite the tone of voice that he used. Although he was earnest, he was also hesitant. It was as though he wasn't sure it was right to ask me to interrupt the obviously more important things that I was doing. I had met the Senator only twice before, once when we participated in a symposium together and once when I talked with him during the course of my study of educational and cultural policy. He had the same quality of diffidence in him today that I had noticed on those earlier occasions. I think that perhaps he places too high a value on what most scholars do and undervalues his own work.

I was stubborn. I mentioned the book I was working on, the attractions of my present existence, my worries about the recent developments in foreign policy. I brought up both the Dominican intervention and Vietnam. Fulbright said that the Foreign Relations Committee had barely begun to look into the Dominican affair. His first impression was simply that events had unfolded at a bewildering speed. As for Vietnam, he believed the President was looking for negotiations without preconditions at the earliest possible time. Only a few weeks ago, the Senator had said this in the Senate. The situation, he thought, was an extremely fluid one. He reminded me that the President was mainly interested in matters like education and welfare, and had every reason not to get deeply involved in a war.

"Perhaps you can persuade the President to try some ideas of yours as alternatives," the Senator said, looking at me over the top of his glasses. I couldn't tell if he thought I could, or hoped I could, or was only teasing me gently. I couldn't tell whether

I was taking him seriously or merely wishing I could.

"Senator," I said, "I need this job like I need a hole in the head."

"I know what you mean about a hole in the head," he said, smiling. "I've been in the Senate twenty years."

I think that was the remark that came closest to persuading me. If he, in that detached and ironic mood, can give twenty years to government and public life, I'm hard put to find a reason why I can't give two or three.

The words were different at the White House, but the melody was much the same: it would be a struggle, but there were unplumbed possibilities in international education. As for the Vietnam affair, no one wanted peace more than the President, and while no one can know what will happen, the President has a way of getting what he wants.

✳

I had a long talk with John Gardner. John has been Chairman of the U.S. Advisory Commission on International Educational and Cultural Affairs, and has been the principal citizens' adviser to the Assistant Secretary for Educational and Cultural Affairs. He thus knows at first hand the situation into which I'm being invited to plunge. John said the job of Assistant Secretary was full of pitfalls and frustrations. There is inadequate understanding in Washington of the nature of the job, a residue of Congressional suspicion toward the entire program, and deep-seated problems of policy and administration; these have made life difficult for everyone who has held the position since the time it was created in 1961. John finished by saying that I ought to do it.

When I said that this sounded like a *non sequitur*, John told me the other side. He had talked with the President last week, and the President's eyes lighted up when education was discussed. Each President, John said, tends to give his own distinctive accent to foreign policy; it would be natural for this

President to accent international education. So I should take the job, despite everything that might go wrong. There was a chance to accomplish something important. President Johnson obviously knew how to get things done: to join his Administration was to have an enormous opportunity for accomplishment. Indeed, if the President ever became really interested in international education, the whole program would be transformed. It could move to the foreground of foreign policy. And even if none of this happened, it would be an experience for me. It would do me good.

*

I ran into Kenneth Galbraith, in Washington for Adlai Stevenson's funeral. He told me that he had been talking to Senator Fulbright about me.

"You must take the job," said Ken. "If I could go to India for a few years, you can come to Washington. It will do you good."

I told Ken that I had some odd, perhaps even quixotic, ideas about foreign policy.

"This President's an old school teacher," said Ken. "He ought to like the kind of thing you represent. Maybe you can give him something more constructive to think about than Vietnam. Anyway, you ought to get into the State Department. It will broaden your horizons. You'll find that it's the kind of organization which, though it does big things badly, does small things badly too."

*

Although I retain some doubts, I find I'm moving toward accepting the job. The position of Assistant Secretary for Cultural Affairs is a troubled one, out at the fringes of the State Department, with no strong constituency behind it, and with a heritage of political and bureaucratic problems. And the Administration's course in the Dominican Republic and Vietnam is disturbing. I don't like what's happening, and

I'm sure that all efforts at long-range change will go on the rocks if the war continues and grows bigger. Still, one has to hope that these have been temporary aberrations. The Administration has compiled an extraordinary record, and particularly in educational legislation. Its main thrust and its whole future seem to me to depend on its continuing in that direction. Why should it destroy itself, particularly when the President himself, in his election campaign, seemed to understand the dangers?

And I've developed a commitment to the ideas in my report. Now that I'm being given even a dim chance to try to put them into effect, how can I turn it down?

✳

I have been talking to various people in Washington who know the lay of the land, and Helen and I have also been looking into apartments and schools. Having thus satisfied myself that I had been methodical in coming to my decision, I called the White House to say that I was beginning to think favorably about undertaking the job. I started to add that I still had some questions about budgetary prospects, Administration attitudes toward the reforms I would hope to make, and other matters, and that I would therefore like the chance for a good brass-tacks discussion, but I never completed what I wanted to say. The White House, I was told, had been trying to reach me all morning. Senator Fulbright had met with the President the evening before, he had brought up my name, and the President had said No. Apparently, his willingness to appoint a man that Senator Fulbright wants doesn't apply to professors of philosophy from New York.

I called Senator Fulbright to thank him and say good-bye. He was a different man from the one I had talked to before. There was flint in his voice. When I told him that I was now, with a measure of relief, going back to New York and the book I had been working on, he became indignant. It was as though

I were telling him that I was defecting. He told me that this
was no time for me to back out. I said that I didn't want a
position that the President had any hesitation about giving
me. He replied that the issue had grown larger than my personal feelings.

Few people, the President included, understood what educational and cultural policy was all about, the Senator said.
They thought it had something to do with show business.
It was time to straighten the whole area out, and I was not
to complicate the matter by withdrawing my name. It was
true that the President had the ultimate right to name the man,
but it took the advice and consent of the Senate to confirm
him. So at least two people had to be satisfied, and maybe more.
The President and he would have another talk, and I was to
sit tight. The only thing I should do was to give him the names
of people he could call to get more information about me.
He had thought my credentials for the job would be immediately evident to the President, and so he had not had all the
supporting information that, it had turned out, he needed.
In particular, he wanted more opinions about my administrative qualifications than he had had the first time around.

Meekly, I gave him what he wanted, and drove back to New
York with Helen.

＊

Senator Fulbright called to say that he hadn't seen the
President yet, and to ask for more names of people who would
know about me. He also said again that I was to do nothing
precipitate like withdrawing my name. It would only make
things worse.

＊

The Democratic Party Chairman in my district called, con-
gratulating me on my appointment. When I told him that his
information was way ahead of mine, he congratulated me for

having learned so quickly how to behave like a public official.

❉

Helen, driving home from the city, stopped to telephone me. She had been listening to the radio; Secretary Celebrezze had retired from the Cabinet to take a federal judgeship, and guess who was the new Secretary of Health, Education and Welfare? I didn't guess. It was John Gardner.

❉

The morning papers carried the full story of John's nomination. I called him. He seemed almost as surprised as I. He had gone in to see the President to deliver a report about the White House Conference on Education, which he had chaired, and the President had put the question to him and asked for an answer quickly. John also said that almost immediately after the public announcement of his nomination, Senator Fulbright had been on the telephone to him, asking about me.

With John in the Cabinet, the prospects for accomplishing something substantial in international education are of course immeasurably better. But quite apart from that, John's appointment is immensely encouraging. It suggests that the President means to make his major moves in the fields of education and welfare.

❉

Speculations differ about the meaning of the President's statements about troop build-up in Vietnam. Is this straightforward escalation, or is the President making a token move, intended to impress the North Vietnamese and to reduce the pressure from the people who want major escalation? I wouldn't know. I suspect that insofar as these speculations are efforts to read the President's long-range intentions, they may all be based on the wrong assumption. The President is quite possibly taking the decisions one at a time, and doesn't know what he will ultimately decide any better than the rest of us.

❋

A telephone call took me away from dinner with Yugoslav friends at the Faculty Club. It was Senator Fulbright. He was the gentle and relaxed man I had first met. He apologized for taking me away from dinner, and told me that he had just seen the President, and that "things are on the track again." All the formal clearance procedures would still have to be gone through, but I ought to hear definitely in a couple of weeks. The Senator sounded very pleased, which pleased me. And though I still have questions about the job, I'm looking forward to it.

3

Plans and Prejudices

In the spring of 1965, having completed a study of American educational and cultural policy abroad which I had undertaken at the request of learned societies and the State Department, I submitted my conclusions, in which I said that the premises of official policy were largely wrong and the government's mode of operation outlandish. Shortly thereafter, I was asked whether I would accept the office of Assistant Secretary of State for Educational and Cultural Affairs.

What were the ideas that I thought should be tried? Their basic premise was that students and professors, writers and artists, scientists and intellectuals, are important social groups, and important politically. It didn't occur to me then, and it doesn't occur to me now, that the people who compose these groups are made of a superior metal. They aren't more responsible, more humane or necessarily more intelligent than people in other walks of life, and the way in which they govern their own institutions gives no reason to suppose that the world would be substantially better governed if they took over. I do not think that "intellectuals"—the term itself is a nest of ambiguities—have special rights in public affairs. But they have the power they have, and that power has implications, whatever the value judgment we pass upon it.

Over the last twenty or thirty years particularly, men of knowledge, professional writers and critics, scholars and artists, have emerged as a social category to which increasing deference is paid and to which growing influence has come. More than ever before, ideas and moral and social attitudes have emanated from the places where these people live and work that deeply affect both domestic and world politics. The relations between societies, and the prospects of any major government's foreign policies, depend, to an extent that has not been adequately understood by those who make foreign policy, on the activities and attitudes of the intellectual community. To push this fact to the foreground, to give it the recognition it deserves, and to develop programs that might give intellectual workers a more active and useful part to play in international affairs was the central purpose to which I wanted to give my attention when I entered the government.

In the summer of 1965, when I suggested that these ideas should be applied in a systematic way to foreign policy, they seemed odder and more debatable than they do now. There had not yet been troubles at Columbia, Harvard and the Sorbonne; Russia's difficulties with its intellectuals had not become fully evident; events in Madrid, Tokyo, Rome, Belgrade and Prague had not yet indicated that something like an international culture of discontent might emerge in the university world. The preoccupations of American foreign policy in the first part of this decade were with projects like establishing a Multi-Lateral Force in Western Europe. In circles where such projects seemed realistic and urgent, discussion of the importance of educational and cultural diplomacy was a little like discussion of the common cold at a meeting of doctors studying diseases of outer space.

Yet it seemed to me that the time was overdue for a change. In the sixteenth century the Spaniards ruined themselves by basing their overseas policies on the premise that gold was wealth. They overlooked, as the British didn't, the significance of commercial power. Similarly, it was a mistake, in this century, I believed, to ignore or misunderstand the role of scientific and intellectual groups. They were pivotal people, on whose attitudes and actions the success of much in domestic policy and in foreign policy turns. The lines going out from the arts, sciences and education have become the life lines for most societies. The arts, in an era of expanding education and rapid communication, have a radiating influence on men's perception of the nature of their environment and of themselves; the sciences are the sources not only of revolutionary technological changes but of views of the world that have put inherited outlooks on the defensive, and have generated, for better or worse, new assessments of the institutions by which men govern their affairs; in all societies, rich or poor, revolutionary or conservative, the school bears an increasingly heavy social role, attempting to fill the gap left by the weakening of the family, the churches and local communities.

And all these areas of activity—the arts, the sciences, education—have particular importance for that segment of the population in contemporary societies which is growing most dramatically in numbers and influence—the youth. A politics, foreign or domestic, which neglects their attitudes or their special institutions has, I was convinced, a shaky future. The universities, in particular, are crucial institutions. They are more than sources of expertise, reservoirs of technical talent needed by a technical society. They house, in a secular age, the new priests, the tutors of the public conscience. It is in the universities, more than anywhere else, that modern societies develop their consciousness of themselves and their moral estimate of their performance.

The practical reforms that I hoped to bring about were based on the conviction, therefore, that some of the fundamental conditions of power, national and international, had been changed. Internally, each nation's strength and cohesiveness depended as never before on the capacity of its educational system to serve as a center of social authority, unification and regeneration. Externally, the relative power of nations was affected more than ever by their ability to win the tolerance and sympathy of the intellectual classes, abroad as well as at home. Most important of all, the new role of the intellectual classes had made the old game of national rivalry suspect.

"*Les honnêtes gens qui pensent*, whatever their nationality," said Voltaire in the eighteenth century, "share the same principles and constitute a single republic." He exaggerated the facts in his own day, and the remark remains an exaggeration in ours. *Les honnêtes gens qui pensent* are not always honest, they do not always think, and national and ideological divisions among them are severe. And yet there are common problems and standards of workmanship that tie chemists, musicians or economists together, whatever their national origins or ideological affinities. In their cooperative pursuits they form international communities, in seed or in full fruition.

Foreign policy must meet new requirements, I felt, when it is conducted within a civilization whose intellectual and educational leaders, on both sides of most political boundaries, have come to look upon such boundaries as increasingly artificial and inconvenient. A government, to be sure, could set its face against such attitudes and even try to control or redirect them. If it was a free government in a free society, however, its chances of making this policy work were minimal. It would merely alienate its intellectual and educational leaders if it tried. On the other hand, it could make a bet on another possibility. It could try to facilitate and encourage the further development of the network of intellectual and cultural partnerships across the borders, and thus use its power to strengthen rather than defeat the conditions making for the gradual evolution of an international political community. The United

States government, the richest and most powerful of all, had a peculiarly good chance to lead the way, it seemed to me, and a special self-interest in doing so.

Arrayed against this approach there existed certain habits of mind, which had taken root inside the government, and which I hoped to loosen a bit. Basically, three points of view prevailed within the government, and had prevailed for twenty years or more, with regard to educational and cultural affairs.

The first was the approach of the hard-nosed psychological warrior. It conceives of educational and cultural activities essentially as forms of propaganda. The purpose of educational and cultural policy, from this point of view, is simply to reach people who have an important role in forming public opinion and to warm them up, whether with a good lecture or a song and dance. Then they will work with us and not against us, and their compatriots will come to see things as we do in international affairs. This, essentially, was the position of the people in charge of the United States Information Agency, the agency responsible for official American information and public-relations activities overseas. Exchanges of students and teachers, the establishment and maintenance of American libraries abroad, international meetings of learned societies or writers' groups, visits of artists and scientists, all these, from this point of view, are activities in which the government of the United States is interested only because they serve the purpose of winning friends and influencing people.

This point of view seemed to me more than crass. It struck me as naïve. When, in the course of my study, I called on one of the principal officials of the Information Agency, he said to me, "The American taxpayer isn't spending money to advance the arts and sciences or to promote anything so intangible as international understanding. He wants good hard results. He wants the national interest to be served." But it seemed to me that "the national interest"—elusive phrase—

might include the advancement of the arts and sciences and the promotion of international understanding. It also seemed to me—in fact, I went home and looked it up, and found I was right—that laws passed by Congress explicitly said that international understanding was a goal of cultural policy. But my disagreement with this view also stemmed from a basic practical consideration. Simple realism suggested that the terms of a workable *modus vivendi* with the intellectual community needed to be understood. That community plays the major role in cultural exchanges, and few of its members are going to go along willingly with a public-relations counselor's view of their function.

The second point of view toward international educational and cultural activities was the technician's. It prevailed in the Agency for International Development, which has primary responsibility for the government's foreign assistance programs. This approach held that educational and cultural activities are primarily instruments for producing the trained manpower that other countries need and thus promoting their economic progress. I thought it closer to the truth than the view that cultural diplomacy is a form of psychological warfare, but I also thought it a limited point of view.

Terms like "technology" and "industrialization" stand for more than machinery, special know-how and the accumulation of capital. They stand for habits of mind and for attitudes toward what is proper as a style of life. The purely technical approach to modernization ignores the cultural context which is needed to sustain economic development. Moreover, it tends to force-fit educational planning, which is a long-range affair, to the Procrustean bed of short-range economic plans aiming at more immediate, dramatic results. While educational plans cannot be made without regard to the economic resources and prospects of a society, the approach of those concerned with specific projects for economic improvement too often tends to ignore the general catalytic effects of educational progress on an entire economy. Education, it seemed to me, had always been unduly submerged in AID's programs of economic assistance.

And there was another point of equal importance. The purely technical approach to foreign assistance pays too little attention to the fact that the export of American know-how can be easily viewed in other countries either as a tactless intrusion or as a conscious moral aggression. It tends to ignore the requirement that Americans, if they are to work usefully with other people, must develop a capacity to tune in on assumptions and values not their own. Although many of the top officials in AID recognized these facts, a narrower doctrine dominated most of our actual programs in developing countries. Programs of cultural exchange, programs aimed at making Americans and their foreign counterparts more sensitive to the nuances of international cooperation, seemed to me a necessary precondition and complement of economic assistance.

The third point of view toward educational and cultural exchange was the view of those seeking "mutual understanding" between nations. They believed that the purpose of educational and cultural relations is to give people more perspective, on themselves as much as on others. Just as the Rhodes Scholarships strengthened good relations between Great Britain and the United States, a broader program might strengthen our relations with other nations. Senator Fulbright, who has had as much to do with the development of a cultural policy for the United States as anyone, held this view. It was shared by many of his colleagues on the Senate Committee on Foreign Relations, and by a number of the most sophisticated and experienced people in the Department of State.

I thought it a civilized view, and a realistic one. All that made it unrealistic was that the Congress and the executive branch had never been persuaded to support it on the proper scale. Under the pressure of the cold war and of preoccupation with economic assistance to the poor countries, this point of view had always been submerged.

But I had also come to think, as a consequence of my study, that the phrase "mutual understanding" gives only a small indication of the nature of the problems posed by educational and cultural policy. These problems are similar to others in international affairs. They have to do with the rectification of imbalances of intellectual power; with the removal of hindrances to communication and negotiation; with the control of cultural aggression, witting or unwitting; with the creation of institutions and enterprises in which there is an international stake, so that the edge is taken off international hostilities and the reasons for keeping peace are multiplied. The phrase "mutual understanding" only begins to suggest the importance, complexity and fascinations of cultural foreign policy, rightly conceived.

Educational and cultural diplomacy is not simply an exercise in the spreading of good will. It has, or should have, quite specific purposes. A first purpose should be to develop arrangements, technical and human, that will lead to a more equitable distribution in the world of ideas and information. There ought to be facilities for the regularized, efficient dissemination of knowledge that would insure that the necessary kind of knowledge goes to the people who need it, and would allow them to tap into the immense reserves of knowledge that have been built up in a few central places in the world, most particularly in the United States. What was needed, I thought (and what is still needed, I think), is what might be called an international knowledge-bank. And to this the United States could make a major contribution.

The United States could act to prevent a kind of tragedy which is today a daily occurrence. There are people suffering in one part of the world because they do not have the answer to problems, in plant husbandry, human medicine or dozens of other areas, which people in another part of the world, and sometimes just across the mountains, have successfully solved.

Much of the time this kind of tragedy is avoidable. Through better provision for the distribution of books, through libraries, information-retrieval systems and computerized networks for the communication of knowledge, through the development of arrangements across the borders that would bring together educational, technical, agricultural or medical organizations to make a concerted attack on common problems, a basic imbalance in the world—the different positions of different nations in relation to their access to what is known—can be partially rectified. Efforts such as this might well contribute as much to the economic development of the poorer countries as straightforward dosages of money and machinery, and would do more to encourage a sense of national independence and accomplishment.

Nor need such efforts to correct imbalances in the distribution of knowledge be directed only toward the poorer countries. In our relations with Great Britain, for example, the so-called "technological gap" has been a troublesome issue. Yet most of the technological knowledge we develop is available, in theory, to the British. What is needed to make it more easily available in practice is a sophisticated system for channeling it to the people who need it. Cooperation in the development of such a system between the United States and Great Britain —and, more broadly, between the United States and the countries of Western Europe—would not by itself eliminate the technological gap, but it would help, and it would alleviate the suspicion that the United States is indifferent to this gap and perhaps even favors its existence.

Equally important in rectifying the imbalance of intellectual resources is the promotion of greater equality of educational opportunity around the world. This is a second purpose of cultural foreign policy. Economic assistance fails to grapple with one aspect of the problem of inequality. It may give people more food, more health, more hope, but it also often exacerbates their feelings of inequality by increasing their country's dependence on its foreign patrons, and its vulnerability to their economic and cultural power. A necessary supplement to economic assistance, therefore, and, in some cases, a substitute for it, is assistance through educational and cultural exchange.

Programs devoted to the promotion of educational and cultural relations provide a context in which Americans can meet others as students and not only as teachers, as beneficiaries and not only as benefactors. Such programs reduce the tutelary relationship that mars our contacts with foreign countries. More than this, they might help reduce one of the basic causes of the inequality of nations—namely, the migration of educated people from the poor countries to the richer ones. Properly replanned, the classic techniques of international cultural diplomacy—regularized exchanges of teachers and students, partnerships between universities in different countries, international meetings—can be used to make opportunities for education and intellectual nourishment in the poorer countries more like those available to people in richer countries.

I thought the experiment, in any case, was worth trying. The answer to the so-called "brain drain" should be sought not in prohibitions against migration, which limit the fundamental right of individuals to live where they desire, but in an affirmative effort to encourage an international circulation of brains. If the United States government were prepared to approach educational cooperation with other countries as an educational problem to be treated in its own proper terms, rather than in terms of propaganda or narrow technical assistance, it might help other countries develop their own training grounds for leadership.

This brings me to a third purpose that I had in mind for a reformed American cultural diplomacy—the development, in schools and in the intellectual circles that have long-range influence over the formation of people's opinions and attitudes, of the *habit* of international cooperation. Could arrangements be made so that two, three or four universities in different countries shared common faculties? Could the United Nations Educational, Scientific and Cultural Organization perhaps create an international teaching corps, to which each nation would contribute, and which would rotate its members through the schools of different nations? Could scholars and teachers from several countries be brought together to look at the textbooks used in their different national school systems, and eliminate at least the grosser forms of misinformation and prejudice in them?

I did not imagine that any of this would be easy. But the international atmosphere would be brisker and more hopeful if serious effort were made to try some of these ideas. A major commitment by the United States government to international education could be just the spark that was needed, it seemed to me, to ignite such an effort at international intellectual disarmament.

But there was one final problem. Little of this could work, I was inclined to think, unless there was a change of orientation in the American government's approach to educational and cultural relations. The emphasis was usually on what we were doing for others, or to them. We were assisting them, enlightening them, correcting their erroneous views of us, helping them to learn to like us. This was the way the Congressional Appropriations Committees usually viewed cultural relations, and many people in the executive branch, including a good portion of those actually involved in the day-to-day work of superintending cultural relations, approached them in the same spirit. It is natural, it need hardly be said, that this should be so. Americans are competitive, and the cold war has encouraged them in this attitude. And it is not unusual, after all, for people to look with pride on their own culture, and to feel that it does no harm to teach others about it. The British, the French, the Germans, the Russians, all use cultural diplomacy to enhance the reputation and prestige of their countries. But the United

States government, it seemed to me, did not need to be quite so assertive in this respect as it usually was.

Our government, I thought, might understand that even a whisper from America can sound like a shout elsewhere, and that, in any case, America didn't usually whisper. The United States is large, powerful and industrially advanced. Even when the drive toward industrialization in other countries has no American impetus behind it, the changes that take place in them in consequence of industrialization have an "American" quality to them. The divisions that arise within societies going through this painful process, the hard choices that are forced upon them, the doubts they feel as they see cherished values disappear, can be laid at the door of the aggressive American colossus. This may or may not be fair, but it is a fact of life, and in such circumstances much depends on the tone or style of American diplomacy. The United States, I believed, needed a diplomacy less brash and impatient.

"Quiet diplomacy" was the style and the mood to which my ideas belonged. Was it a possible style, a possible mood, for the United States of America? Our culture has its charms, but tranquillity and self-effacement are not among them. In Rome the American Embassy dominates the main street. In London it takes over a main square of its own. In Paris it backs up against the residence of the President of the Republic. Given the condition of the world, we would be front and center even if we didn't try; but we try. Even though we're Number One, we keep trying harder.

When our government has a proposal to make to other governments, it makes sure, as probably no other government does, that its proposal will not be rejected for lack of a hearing. It tries to insure that every explanation has been given, every medium of communication employed, every willing ear reached. American officials do this, so far as I can see, for the simplest of reasons. They want to be able to say to themselves, and to report to Washington, that they have really done their best to put a message across. But while this builds up self-esteem, I am not sure it persuades others. Particularly in the area of cultural relations, I felt, what was needed was less bureaucracy and less hustle, a less conspicuous government presence and a less conspicuous American presence.

Not that this is easy to bring about. Even if Americans could learn the virtues of a less obtrusive diplomacy, the world often conspires against it. One of the distinguished career officers in the United States Foreign Service, a man who has served as ambassador in an important post, has felt for years that, in our diplomacy, we do things clumsily: we make too much noise; we are too eager for results; we act as though there were no tomorrow. He thinks it would be better if we took it easier, letting history work its slow ways and perhaps giving events a tactful nudge from time to time. The Ambassador, in fact, finally got around to writing an essay on the subject, which he called "Quiet Diplomacy." He had just completed it when a mob came along and stormed his embassy, forcing him to burn the essay, along with the other papers. As his story suggests, the facts of international life aren't always compatible with quiet diplomacy. Nevertheless, on the assumption that Aristotle is right, and that men strike a golden mean by leaning over backward away from their natural vices, quiet diplomacy seems to me, on the whole, the right style for the United States.

But the prospects for such a style, rest, in the end, on a change in what American schools, colleges and universities do —a change in what they do not simply in programs concerned directly with international affairs, but in their general curricula, and in the day-to-day experience they provide their students and teachers. It seeemed to me, when I was reflecting on whether I should enter the government, that American cultural diplomacy could be a means to the internationalizing of that experience, and to the broadening of American perspectives. We could not escape our position in the world: we would have to educate ourselves up to it.

Programs in international education and cultural exchange seemed to me, in this way, to be programs for the improvement of American education. "The most happy of mortals should I think myself," wrote Montesquieu in his preface to *The Spirit of Laws*, "could I contribute to make mankind recover from their prejudices. By prejudices I here mean, not that which renders men ignorant of some particular things, but whatever renders men ignorant of themselves."

The elementary function of international education, in the United States or any other country, is to render men less ignorant of themselves. I thought I would like to see what could be done to put into practice the idea that a better foreign policy for the future might start in the American classroom.

But all this takes me to more mundane matters—specifically, to bureaucracy. In coming into the government, I had had more than abstract ideas in mind. I hoped to produce a practical change in the way that educational and cultural affairs were administered. The theory and style of the hard sell were firmly installed in the government; they had squatters' rights in the extraordinary system—really a nonsystem—by which the government conducted educational and cultural relations. To change that system was going to be the hardest practical prob-lem I would face.

To explain this problem, I must describe the peculiar history of educational and cultural affairs in the United States government. It is a zigzag and confusing history, and its details may not interest the reader who has been lured this far by the promise that he would simply be told what an experience inside the government is like. Such a reader can skip this section of my story without missing anything essential. Nevertheless, it is possible that the history I am about to recount will prove in-structive. For it does illustrate what I am half-inclined to think may be a fundamental Law of Government. It is this: *Whatever happens in government could have happened differently, and it usually would have been better if it had.* And to this law there is also a corollary: *Once things have happened, no matter how accidentally, they will be regarded as manifestations of an unchangeable Higher Reason.* For every argument inside government that some jerry-built bureaucratic arrangement should be changed, there are usually twenty arguments to show that it rests on God's own Logic, and that tampering with it will bring down the heavens.

This law and its corollary are exemplified in the creation and continued existence of the mechanisms that govern the operation of educational and cultural programs as a regular part of American foreign policy. Until the end of 1952 these programs were the responsibility of an Assistant Secretary of State who was also responsible for the United States information program overseas. In 1953 John Foster Dulles, no doubt stimulated in part by the fact that Senator Joe McCarthy had the information activities of the State Department in his gunsights, decided that the Department should get rid of these responsibilities. Mr. Dulles proposed to create a new agency outside the Department of State, and to give it the duty of conducting both information programs and cultural programs.

However, at this point the Senate intervened. Led by Senators Bourke Hickenlooper and William Fulbright, it passed a resolution which asserted that the objectives of educational and cultural programs were different from those of information programs, and that the two should therefore be administered separately. In consequence, the Department of State took the educational and cultural programs back under its wing. Thus an initial oddity in the administration of cultural affairs was produced. In terms of the efficient administration of foreign policy, if the Department of State were faced with a choice of retaining direct control of either educational programs or information programs, it would have made more sense to have retained the information programs.

But the reverse took place. Although the argument is surely

more persuasive that information programs should be responsive to the day-to-day tactical demands of foreign policy,
these were placed in a separate agency. In contrast, cultural
programs, which benefit not at all from seeming to be under
the authority of the same people who have to decide about
military alliances or votes in the UN, were made the business
of the State Department. (Happily, the State Department has
usually accorded considerable autonomy to these programs.
Nevertheless, their connection with the State Department invites misinterpretations of their function, administrative confusion and occasional ham-handed efforts to bend them to
short-range political purposes.)

On the whole, however, the decision to keep educational and
cultural programs within the Department of State was a workable one, so far as it went. Its shortcoming was that it was only
a half-completed decision. The Senate had said that cultural
programs should be separated from information programs, but
it had not said what should be done about the people who had
worked on both these kinds of program in the State Department, and who now had to be divided between two organizations. The bureaucracy got to work on this knotty problem.
After six months of negotiation, in order to reach a compromise,
it adopted a simple rule-of-thumb: All the people involved
were neatly divided into two classes, those who were abroad
and those who were in Washington. Those abroad were assigned
to the new Information Agency, and those in Washington were
kept in the Department of State. In consequence, the cultural
section of the State Department was deprived of representatives of its own overseas. To find such representatives it had
no place to turn but to the Information Agency. Cultural Affairs Officers, employees of the Information Agency, became
the administrators abroad of the American cultural program.
This is the situation that still exists. The State Department,
and not the Information Agency, pays the salaries of these
officers, but it neither hires nor fires nor assigns them.

Thus did bureaucracy "solve" the problem. The Senate had wanted cultural affairs sharply separated from propaganda activities. The bureaucracy came up with a solution that put cultural affairs overseas in the hands of people whose primary mission, as members of the Information Agency, was propaganda. The Senate had wanted the State Department to be responsible for cultural policy. But the Assistant Secretary for Cultural Affairs, given the rules that prevail in bureaucracies, cannot communicate directly with Cultural Affairs Officers who are presumably carrying out his policies, nor can they do so with him. The man who sits in between is the chief of the Information Service in the embassy (the Public Affairs Officer, so called). This officer, whose background is usually in the mass media or public relations, directly supervises the Cultural Affairs Officer, evaluates his performance, and makes the fundamental decisions that affect his advancement in the Information Service. I suspect there are few more frustrating jobs in the United States government than that of Cultural Affairs Officer. Fortunately, the work is intrinsically interesting, but, even so, recruiting good people for the position isn't easy. Its built-in confusions and conflicts are too great.

Nor do the complications stop here. What is culture, and what is information? It may interest the reader to learn that "culture," in the foreign policy circles of the United States government, refers to what *people* communicate, while "information" refers to what *things* communicate. For purposes of bureaucratic convenience, the rule was established that the cultural division of the State Department would deal with students, teachers, researchers, athletes, performing artists, while the Information Service would have jurisdiction over books, libraries, films, television and the visual arts. One would imagine that the latter were also necessary and useful parts of a rounded and coherent international cultural program. But in imagining this, one does not focus on the problems that were faced by a bureaucracy trying to divvy up bureaucratic property. It needed definitions that would clearly mark out the different jurisdictions of the two new agencies and leave no room for evasion. Whether a rational program could be developed in terms of such definitions was a secondary question.

This, then, was the practical situation which I hoped to do something to correct by entering the government. If it was not an impossible situation in which to introduce a new conception of educational and cultural diplomacy, it was a quite difficult one. And the underlying issue posed by this situation transcended mere considerations of administrative efficiency and rationality. It had to do with the general drift of American foreign policy, and with the relation of the government to the intellectual community.

Surely I did not imagine that by reforming bureaucracies or redefining the purposes of educational and cultural exchanges the respect and confidence of the intellectual community could be won. A government's general policies—its weakness for unilateral military intervention, for example—can do more to alienate international intellectual opinion than the best-devised programs in educational and cultural affairs can repair. But it did seem to me that if educational and cultural affairs were properly organized, a center of initiative and a point of view might emerge in one area of foreign policy whose influence might spread to other areas. At the very least, the government had the opportunity, in the field of educational and cultural affairs, to begin to redress its relations to people without whose support the country could not be governed well.

The government could not indefinitely continue to treat intellectuals, scientists, artists and educators simply as people to be used; it could not persist in ignoring their curious mores, and their ingrown suspicion of official power and governmental manipulation, without eventually making a problem for itself as severe as a quarrel with organized labor. To my mind, the government faced a fundamental issue, and its approach to international educational and cultural affairs was part of that issue: Would it push the intellectual and educational world still farther away from it, or would it find ways to give that world a sense that it might participate in public enterprises it respected? On the answer which the American government gave to that question I thought that rather large consequences rode. A government which antagonizes its intellectual constituency ends not only by making a problem for itself. It ends by deepening the gulf between intellect and power, between "the system" and its watchmen and critics. It thus helps to freeze the society it governs into self-distrust and self-alienation. The chance to do something to resist such a process or to reverse it seemed to me a substantial reason to enter the government.

4

Settling Down: Excerpts from a Log

August, 1965:

The White House has asked a small group of officials to put together educational proposals for the next session of Congress. Frank Keppel, the Commissioner of Education, called me from Washington to ask if I would work up the recommendations in international education.

Frank said that he hoped the rumors were true that I was coming into the government, but that the White House wanted me to do the job in any case.

I agreed to do it. As for my nomination as Assistant Secretary, I've still to hear final word, or indeed any word, since the call from Senator Fulbright.

*

I've completed the memorandum and delivered it to Frank in Washington. It's ambitious; I shall be pleased and surprised if the Administration buys even a part of it.

The most important recommendation is for legislation to provide long-term grants to colleges and universities to help them develop new programs in international education. The grants would not commit institutions to perform particular missions for the government; they would be made to assist the renovation of curricula and the strengthening of faculties in the interest of the institutions' basic educational programs. Indeed, "international education," as I use the phrase, doesn't mean only international studies in the technical sense; it means an enlarged international perspective in education generally.

As a by-product, this legislation would also provide the basis for a more substantial and better-organized exchange program abroad. The grants would make it possible for American colleges and universities to enter into cooperative arrangements with institutions overseas. Exchange programs could thus become the direct responsibility of educational institutions, and the government bureaucracy would play a more subordinate role than it now does. This would also help to take educational and cultural relations out of the orbit of the State Department or the Information Agency. My recommendation is that HEW have full authority for this new grant program. The Department of State should obviously not take on a domestic educational responsibility of this sort.

The memorandum also recommended the creation of a corps of "Education Officers," to be attached to our embassies abroad. Although they will be subject to the authority of the ambassador when they are overseas, their long-term affiliation would be with HEW. Their mission will be to facilitate the activities emerging from the new legislation, and to represent the American educational community at large. If adopted, this proposal will end the subordination of international education to public relations.

If the President accepts the proposals in the memorandum, and if Congress acts on them favorably, the federal government will have done more than give financial support to higher education. It will have put its moral authority behind efforts to reduce the parochialism of American schools, and will have found a new and solider ground on which to base the giving of long-term assistance to higher education: the assistance will be given not to meet an emergency, or to buy specific services, but for the straightforward reason that the country has a permanent educational interest in understanding and cooperating with other countries.

The memorandum also recommended that the President give a major speech indicating his desire to make international education central in foreign policy. I am told that in October he may have an opportunity to deliver such a speech at Princeton.

In talking to one of the President's assistants some days ago, I asked him what the prospects for these ideas were, and he was moderately optimistic. He thought that international education was just the sort of thing that might get the President's attention, and that if it did there were immense possibilities. Education was at the center of the President's domestic program, and he was eager to give foreign policy his distinctive stamp. But the President's man added that, of course, if this Vietnam affair should grow larger, all bets were off. I suggested that this was one more reason not to let the affair grow worse. "That," he said, "is unfortunately not up to us."

The war will be less and less something we can control if it goes on. But one has to take a chance on the proposition that the Administration's Vietnam policy is a temporary aberration, a kind of hangover from the past, and that it intends to find a way out fast. The President's domestic record is extraordinary, and the whole future of his Administration seems to me to depend on his continuing the efforts he has made in the fields of welfare and education. It makes no sense for this Administration to turn its back on its successes and become trapped by a war of such doubtful validity and prospects. The President's campaign last fall suggests he recognizes this, and Senator Fulbright has told me that he leans toward this view of the President's intentions. The recent appointment of John Gardner to HEW offers evidence, I think, that the President intends to make his major moves in the cities and the schools. In any case, nothing will be accomplished by my assuming the worst. The moment may not be perfect for the recommendations I've made, but I don't know when it's ever been better.

＊

The White House announced yesterday that the President had nominated me to be Assistant Secretary of State. In Washington, a note from Dean Rusk was waiting for me at my hotel. I called and went over to see him. I had last seen him in 1960, when he was President of the Rockefeller Foundation. He didn't seem very changed, and was still soft-spoken and unpretentious. We talked about ways and means of keeping communications open between us, about the management of my bureau, and about Congressional relations. The Secretary said that Congress was a representative body of men, perhaps somewhat superior to the average. Of course, there was a fringe of difficult people, as in all groups—perhaps 10 or 15 percent. I reminded him that I came from a university faculty: if only 10 or 15 percent of the people in Congress were difficult, I felt that, with my background, I might find the situation quite manageable.

＊

My confirmation hearing before the Senate Foreign Relations Committee was held today. Senator Javits called the committee to support my nomination, and Robert Kennedy, whom I had never met before, introduced me to the committee. He said that the job for which I was being considered was, to his mind, one of the most important in the whole range of our foreign efforts, and that the President had made an excellent nomination.

Senators Hickenlooper and Lausche asked me a number of questions about my membership on the Board of Directors of the Civil Liberties Union. Senator Hickenlooper said that he thought the Civil Liberties Union was rather like a left-wing version of the John Birch Society, and asked me where I would put it on the political spectrum. I tried to answer in a quiet, informational voice, and said that, while I didn't always agree with the positions the organization took, I thought that, in principle, it stood dead center, on the Constitution and the Bill of Rights. We avoided fireworks. But I thought I heard Senator Kennedy, who was sitting in the row of seats just behind me, whispering, "Incredible! Incredible!" as this line of questioning proceeded. I think Senator Hickenlooper may have heard him too, which probably didn't help.

I called the White House to report about the hearings and told them that Robert Kennedy had introduced me. They seemed interested and surprised.

September, 1965:

I have come down to Washington ahead of Helen and the children, and went to work today. The confirmation of my appointment by the Senate still hasn't come through.

The most important event of this first official day at work was a call from the White House. The President is to deliver a major address next week at the bicentennial celebration at the Smithsonian Institution, and I was asked to prepare a draft. I could not have had better news. The speech that I had hoped the President would give later in the fall can be given immediately. Nothing will be more useful than to get the feeling going, as soon as I can, that action and change are taking place.

✻

I brought a draft of the Smithsonian speech over to the White House. Fortunately, the President's staff can turn it into his speech. I don't have the reflexes of a ghost writer. Nevertheless, when I left the White House after discussing the draft, I had the impression that the basis of the speech was there. The draft puts the President unmistakably on the line with respect to the launching of a new program in international education.

＊

I received from the White House a rewritten draft of the Smithsonian Address. The basic ideas, the sequence of thought and many of the key phrases from my draft remain unchanged, but this version is happily shorter—the words and sentences, as well as the speech as a whole. The principal alterations are in tone and emphasis. The tone is more expansive, and greater prominence is given to the U.S. government's desire to do something about the problem of illiteracy in the world. The rhetoric is populist: there are references to the more than 700 million adults who "dwell in darkness where they cannot read or write."

Reviewing the draft, I wished that it had retained just a bit more of its original stress on educational exchange. The present version carries a heavier implication of one-way educational assistance from us to others. But the idea that an international education program involves a process of give-and-take remains, though it isn't as prominent. I also worried over broad phrases that might seem to promise too much, and I was concerned, at first, about the degree of emphasis given to illiteracy. Great publicity given to a drive against illiteracy invites educational demagogy. Specious statistical gains—the number of people that pass reading tests—tend to become the main preoccupation, without regard to whether or not literates have anything to read or what they take from their reading. Moreover, attention and resources can be diverted from the main task of educating the young to what I think should be a subordinate effort to teach reading to people of all ages. My own belief is that the major effort in most poor countries, at the moment, should be in secondary education. This is where the teachers will be trained, and it is the place to begin to improve the quality of primary education.

But, of course, I'm reading too much into the draft, which doesn't deny any of these points. The speech is ambitious, and it leaves plenty of room for the development of a rounded program. It is certainly an improvement over my version. This draft commits the President to take action even more firmly than my original draft did. It's an excellent beginning.

❋

I was sworn in today and have stopped supporting the government with free labor. George Ball officiated and made some charming and perspicacious remarks. I was also told that it looks as though the President will give the Smithsonian speech tomorrow in the form in which I last saw it.

Today, in the Senate, Senator Fulbright delivered a speech too. He condemned the Administration for its intervention in the Dominican rebellion last spring. The impact at the White House and over here at the State Department is rather as though a bomb fell. Indignation and anger are the major reactions.

❋

The President delivered the speech at the Smithsonian convocation. His tone was flat, and the people around me, representing more than eighty countries, seemed not to be listening. Perhaps it was the heat. Unfortunately, the *Times* is on strike, so the speech won't get the coverage we had hoped for.

The President's face surprised me by its sternness. Was it, perhaps, because Fulbright was also there on the platform? But the President did give the speech, and we now have a program on which to proceed. The key passages, to my mind, are the following:

In our country and in our time we have recognized with new passion that learning is basic to our hopes for America. . . .

But the legacy we inherit from James Smithson cannot be limited to these shores. He called for the increase and diffusion of knowledge among men, not just Americans, not just Anglo-Saxons, and not just the citizens of the Western world—but all men everywhere.

We know today that . . . ideas, not armaments, will shape our lasting prospects for peace; that the conduct of our foreign policy will advance no faster than the curriculum of our classrooms; and that the knowledge of our citizens is the treasure which grows only when it is shared. . . .

That is why I have directed a special task force within my Administration to recommend a broad and long-range plan of worldwide educational endeavor. . . .

First, to assist the education effort of the developing nations and the developing regions.

Second, to help our schools and universities increase their knowledge of the world and the people who inhabit it.

Third, to advance the exchange of students and teachers who travel and work outside their native lands.

Fourth, to increase the free flow of books and ideas and art, of works of science and imagination.

And, fifth, to assemble meetings of men and women from every discipline and every culture to ponder the common problems of mankind.

In all these endeavors, I pledge that the United States will play its full role.

By January, I intend to present such a program to the Congress. . . .

＊

I had a meeting in my office today to go over the practical implications of the Smithsonian Address. I detected a variety of attitudes. The people in CU who've been concerned with long-range policy planning seemed full of pep at the prospect. The more administrative types, responsible for taking care of what exists, were neither favorable nor unfavorable. They somehow gave the impression that the meeting was an interruption of more important business. The budget people were interested and attentive, and were also fundamentally unconvinced that anything was going to happen.

The Fulbright speech on the Dominican intervention came up in the course of calls from the White House. The indignation about it continues. One man told me that everybody knew that I was an old friend of the Senator's, so I would have to be careful about what I did and said because I was skating on thin ice. I replied, in the quiet, informational tone of voice that I have learned to employ, that I admired the Senator, but that I hadn't known him before he began to push for my appointment, and that I neither owed him any special favors nor had he ever even faintly suggested that I did. My interlocutor at the other end of the phone was greatly surprised. Since the Senator worked hard for my appointment, the inference has been that we must be old cronies. I am told that there are even people at the White House who think I came originally from Arkansas. Well, there are reporters here who think I came from Texas. It's that kind of town.

❋

Dean Rusk asked me about Fulbright today, but not about the Dominican speech. He asked whether I knew what Fulbright's attitude was going to be toward the new international education program. I said that the Senator had seemed sympathetic when I spoke to him, and had warned only that it must not be a missionary program. The Secretary seemed to agree with this advice.

❋

My office is beginning to receive a substantial number of inquiries from foreign embassies, American universities and educational organizations, asking for more information about the implications of the Smithsonian Address.

❋

Senator Fulbright and I lunched together today. I wanted
to talk to him about the President's speech and what it could
mean, but his mind was on other things. He talked about his
Dominican speech, saying that he had been advised by some
of the people around him not to give it because it was ill-timed.
But he had thought he ought to deliver it, since it might help
in a small way to discourage the Administration from further
adventures of that sort.

The Senator talked about the feelings of people from poor
parts of the world. His own state, Arkansas, was one of the poor
sections of the country, and, after the Civil War, it had learned
what it meant to live under the occupation and tutelage of people from the outside. No matter how smart the outsiders were,
they made mistakes and they were resented. That was why
something like the Dominican intervention was the wrong
course to follow. He ended by saying that he also wasn't sure
what we were doing in Vietnam.

❋

We now have the final membership list for the Task Force
on International Education. Its membership will be secret. This
may make it easier to keep the membership of the Task Force
essentially professional, and to resist pressures to make appointments for political reasons. It also leaves the President freer
to take or leave what the Task Force recommends.

❋

This morning, I had a talk, almost a scrimmage, with Vice
President Humphrey. I had learned that the people in CU in
charge of the program that sends American lecturers and con-
sultants abroad on special missions had turned down a labor
leader whose reputation, so far as I knew, was excellent. "Ad-
verse information," I was told. The information, when I looked
into it, seemed loose innuendo and not much more. Since the
Vice President was one of those who had written a letter of

reference for the man, and appeared to know him well, I thought I would call him. I wanted to have his information about the man so that I could have a better sense of what the people in charge of the program were willing to accept as "evidence," and what their criteria of selection were.

I got through to the Vice President on the telephone, but I barely got my question asked before he let me have it about the stuffiness and timidity of too many people in the State Department. He warmed up so much to the subject that I had to hold the receiver away from my ear: it was as though he were making a speech in a public hall. But he was convincing, both about the merits of the man in question and about the more general theme of State Department conservatism. When he finished, I managed to hold him long enough to tell him that I had telephoned hoping that the call might help change attitudes in the Department. He sounded a little mollified, but not much.

✳

The Arts and Humanities Bill was signed at the White House today. I was there for the ceremony, and then turned up at the Smithsonian in the evening, where, with Roger Stevens and the Vice President, I was a host at the reception celebrating the passage of the bill. While I was ushering the Vice President to the main reception room, he suddenly looked at me earnestly and said that he was sorry to have given me a hard time the day before. I told him that, on the contrary, he had given me some help.

He complained that he lives an insane life. " 'Why am I doing this?' I say to myself when I limp home at two in the morning. I say to Muriel that we ought to change our way of life. All the awful food. All these receptions and talk, talk, talk. I hear they've got a wonderful exhibit right next door, but do you think I'll ever see it? Oh, no. They won't let me."

He pointed to one of his bodyguards. "It's these fellows here.

They tell me I've got to go here and I've got to go there. What's the matter with you, Kelly?" he said, suddenly turning on the man. "Every time I see you, you're at a party! Why don't I have some fun instead of going through these mad whirls, and never eating dinner, and stuffing myself with things like these?" He held up a canapé. "These are delicious, aren't they?"

*

One of my State Department colleagues told me today about the telephone call from the President to inform him of my appointment. He didn't know whether Senator Fulbright was present in the President's office when he made the call, but the President said: "Bill Fulbright wants this appointment. And what Bill Fulbright wants, Bill Fulbright gets."

It's different now, hardly two months later. It's been suggested that, at least for a while, I would be wise to keep any new initiatives in international education as separate as possible from "the Fulbright program." The name makes some people prickly.

*

This afternoon I finally had the briefing on "security" which the Security Office has been so eager to arrange. I went to the Security Office's corridor at the appointed time. Their briefing officer was late. When he came along, he led me to the door of the briefing room, and after much twisting of dials and insertion of keys in assorted keyholes, he ushered me into a cork-lined room dominated by a large sign saying "No Smoking." The first thing my man did was to take out a cigarette and light it.

The briefing was a little disorganized. The briefing officer's main interest seemed to be in all the new bugging devices. "Some of this stuff is really hairy," he said, his voice muffled as he told me about tiny microphones no larger than buttons that could be hidden in a cigarette package or left unobtrusively on my window sill. He talked as though he had all the time in the world, and as though I did too. Since he wasn't telling me anything I didn't know from reading the public print, I thought that perhaps I had better take charge of the agenda, and I asked him whether there was some special information that he thought I needed—for example, what the classifications "Limited Official Use," "Confidential," "Secret" and "Top Secret" actually meant. Since I was already handling such documents, instruction on this point would be of use to me. He answered that the basic principle to keep in mind was "the need to know": unless a person had a "need to know" certain information, the information shouldn't be given to him.

"And 'the need to know' doesn't mean anything different for each classification?" I asked.

" 'The need to know' means the need to know," he said.

"You're not holding back on me?" I asked. "I mean, the meaning of the different classifications, that isn't itself classified information, is it?"

He slowed up, as though it had dawned on him that I was a little dull, and would need a lengthier explanation. "Take your own file," he said. "Naturally, you're a Presidential appointee, so we had a full field investigation of you. There's everything about you in that file, but I mean *everything*. There's nothing about you that we don't know. Naturally, it's very sensitive material. We just can't show it freely to people. The President's seen it maybe, and I have, and one or two others. But you don't have to worry, because we figure that only a very small number of people have a need to know all that stuff about you. Now do you understand what I mean?"

The afternoon was growing long. In a last effort to get an answer to my question, I asked him whether the definitions I was about to give for "Top Secret," "Secret" and the rest were correct. I tried the definitions on him. "Why, yes," he said with surprise. "That's about right. How did you know?"

"Those were the definitions we used when I was in Naval Intelligence," I said to him.

"Were you in Naval Intelligence?" he said. "I didn't know that."

5

A Base of Operations

"Well, how do you like power?" an old friend asked me about a month after I had gone to Washington.

"I like it," I said, "but I hope it likes me."

What I was trying to tell him only became clearer to me as more days and months went by. I think I was trying to say that holding power, at any rate in the government of the United States, isn't like holding a club. It's more like holding an animate thing that needs to be fed and cajoled and has its own life to live. You have to adjust to it. My experience with power, if that is the word for what it was that I had, has helped me to understand a little better the answers to some of the questions that must puzzle any reasonably interested citizen when he looks at the government of his country.

Why is it that the government takes so long to do anything? Why do so many ideas that look bold, new and promising when they go into the government hopper look so tired and flat when they come out? And why are all the energetic, enlightened, optimistic fellows who go into the government telling old friends on the outside, within a month or two, that things can't be changed overnight, and that most of what's going on makes more sense than any outsider can realize? A large part of the answer, I think, lies in the fact that the man who enters government is given power. And that power, although he needs it to translate his thoughts into reality, also imposes limitations on his capacity to do so.

Almost all old hands in government will tell you, as though it were axiomatic, that if you want to accomplish anything in government, you have to have people who work for you, and a budget, and a base of operations. Allowing for exceptional cases in which a man is very close to the President, it won't do, according to the conventional wisdom, simply to have good ideas, or to have important people who turn to you for advice; it isn't even enough to have one of those imposing pieces of paper in your hand known as Executive Orders or Presidential Memoranda, which designate you as the President's specially chosen instrument to carry out his policies. These are pieces of paper. If you want to hoist them to your mast, you had better be riding on a sound ship and have plenty of ballast in the hold. You need an organization; you need troops. In the jargon, you need "clout."

This axiom is a half-truth. The story is told that a visitor once came to the White House and presented an idea to President Kennedy. The President was enthusiastic. "That's a first-rate idea," he said. "Now we must see whether we can get the government to accept it." For while a man needs a base of operations if he is going to accomplish anything, a base of operations is also a drag. Without a base you can't do very much. With such a base you can't do what you thought you could.

Most of what I am about to describe is drawn from my experience in the Department of State, but I suspect that it applies to most branches of government. Certain facts of life are as inevitable in government as dust on one's shoes.

A principal difficulty created by a large base of operations comes simply from the machinery of action on which such a base relies. To be an Assistant Secretary of State is to be in a situation in which other voices speak through you, and you speak through other voices. The letters you sign you usually haven't written. The most important letters you write are those which others sign—the Secretary of State or the President. If you are at a meeting, the chances are that you are quoting from a memorandum that has been prepared for you. When you give a speech, three or four other people, and sometimes thirty or forty, have worried about that speech, often more than you have. Even when you use words that are entirely your own, surprising things happen to them. They go reverberating down corridors, and in and out of other offices, where they become cables to embassies, press releases, policy statements. And although the sound of your voice has been amplified, somewhere along the line it has also been flattened out. Group thinking has intervened, and while the power you have goes much further, it is no longer your power alone.

Indeed, an Assistant Secretary of State who engages in something as commonplace as a telephone conversation is actually enmeshed in an intricate organizational performance. Whenever I talked on the telephone, one person in my outer office, and not infrequently two, listened in. This is standard State Department procedure. It leaves a record of what you have said and of the agreements you have made; and it sets wheels in motion as far as ten thousand miles away without your ever having to give an explicit order. If you say that you will write a letter to Senator X, explaining why his proposed bill to alleviate the "brain drain" is a mistake, that letter, with no further word from you, will be written, and will show up on your desk for your signature. If you intimate that there is something to be said in favor of expediting the visa for that doctor from the Philippines, the doctor may never know what happened to him but he is likely to be on his way to America the next day. This *is* the feel of power. Words have consequences. You think about what you're saying.

And yet it is wrong to describe positions at the top of the

government as "command posts." This is the language that C. Wright Mills used, and others who like to think that they "tell it like it is" use similar language. Like many self-styled "realists," they prefer their facts melodramatic and their story line neat. But the realities are more complex. The machinery at a man's command commands him. If it exists to do his will, he also exists to take care of it.

Before I took my post, it had not occurred to me, for example, that one purpose that was going to be served by my becoming Assistant Secretary of State for Educational and Cultural Affairs was that the Department of State would acquire a new consultant on its space problems. But it did, and the consultant was me. Almost from the moment that I was sworn in, and for more than a year thereafter, I was under pressure from the administrative section of the Department, which wanted to move most of the people in my Bureau to offices outside the building. Almost every month a new order for them to move would come to my desk; almost every month I spent valuable time showing why a move was harmful, offering alternative plans and persuading the administrative people to take their orders back. And it was time, as I observed to myself with some irritation, that was stolen from the preparation of plans for a new International Education Act or from meeting with medical school representatives to discuss the migration of foreign physicians to this country.

Indeed, I spent more than time on the struggle. I spent political capital. When you convince a man on one matter, it's that much harder to convince him on the next. If he decides for you this time, he's likely to think, the next time, that you owe it to him to give in. So I found myself using up capital simply to preserve existing machinery, rather than to promote important policy changes. Nor would it have been sensible for me to delegate these worries about office space to one of my deputies. I did as much of this as I could, but when the chips were down, I had to make the case personally. It was the only way of showing that I thought the issue was important.

And it *was* important: that was what surprised me—that I thought it was. When had I ever cared about office space? But I had come into the government with the hope of moving educational and cultural affairs more to the center of foreign policy, and I would hurt that effort if I allowed the Bureau of Educational and Cultural Affairs to be moved out of the Department's main building. The symbolism, and the effects on the Bureau's morale, would have had too discouraging an impact on the program I was trying to promote.

The care and greasing of machinery imposed many other obligations. It seemed to me, for example, that we could probably not only save money but get a larger amount of useful work done if superfluous jobs in CU were eliminated. When I took office, therefore, I asked the people in charge of personnel in CU to review its staffing pattern, and, after checking with me, to move ahead to cut unnecessary positions. But if the difficulties attached to job-cutting are severe in private business, they are, as I discovered, many times greater in government. Normally, a job can be eliminated only when the occupant retires or is given a new assignment. If I wanted to speed up the slow course of nature, it was usually necessary for me to find another job for the occupant of the superfluous one. Not unnaturally, this generally meant creating a new and superfluous job somewhere else in the Department. In short, I had to find a way to do unto other bureaus what they had previously done unto mine. This process required deals, trades and the incurring of obligations that had nothing directly to do with the purpose that had brought me into the Department. And once again, it took time.

The process of staffing a bureau is as good a way as any to learn some of the basic realities about power in government. To have power is only to have something to trade on. You may want Mr. Jones to work for you because he has experience in just the field you require. Mr. Jones himself wants the assignment. But the reply you get from the Department's personnel director is that perhaps you can get Mr. Jones next year or the year after. Right now, here is Mr. Smith. He has just finished four years in Congo-Brazzaville, and before that he was in Ougadougou. He is tired and his wife's health isn't too good. He is overdue for an assignment in Washington. And he is, after all, a Foreign Service Officer. He should not have too much difficulty, therefore, catching on to the nuances of a job requiring him to understand cultural relations with India.

The arresting point about all this is that, after I had been in the Department hardly a month, I found this kind of reply not unreasonable. Of course, I kept my feelings of sympathy for the problems of personnel officers more or less hidden from view. I followed the advice that Dean Rusk gave me in our first interview, when he brought up the problem of the in-fighting for good people that goes on between the different parts of the State Department: he told me that I would have to use my elbows, and that is what I did. Just the same, I did come to recognize some simple though inconvenient facts. The Department had a career service. If the people in that service were to be reasonably satisfied with their lot in life, the pains and pleasures of membership in it had to be distributed with some effort at even-handedness. Accordingly, there were other considerations to be taken into account, in assigning people to jobs, than the preferences of the heads of bureaus. In fact, the heads of bureaus should be encouraged to develop more educated and responsible preferences.

None of this, after a few months, had to be explained to me. Teamwork can do remarkable things to a man. I had become a member of a team, and I was concerned about its goals and requirements.

Any base of operations is composed of human beings to whom you develop loyalties. A base of operations in the State Department is a particularly close web of loyalties, and sometimes a closed one. It is made up of people who have done difficult things together, who have seen one another tested, and who are bound to one another by memory and sentiment. People who have gone through a crisis in Brazil or Yemen in each other's company, or who have stood side by side under the pummeling of a Congressional Appropriations Committee, come out with feelings toward each other that transcend personal advantage or disadvantage, ideological agreement or disagreement.

This phenomenon of personal loyalty and group solidarity receives less attention in studies of politics and government than the more widely advertised phenomena of disloyalty, backbiting and self-aggrandizement. But it is the source of the richest pleasures of public life, and it is also one of the reasons for the curious phenomenon, which shows up so often, of governmental imperviousness to external influences. On the one side, it gives men psychological support, the joys of a shared experience, the satisfaction of participation in a collective achievement. On the other hand, everybody in one's group or crowd or club can be so busy scratching everybody else's back that people on the outside have trouble breaking through this system of mutual encouragement and reinforcement. The fact that there may be intellectual and moral issues at stake, apart from the issue of loyalty to the people you know, tends to be obscured.

The tendency of an organization to transform itself, for better and worse, into a club is particularly conspicuous in the State Department. The core of the Department consists of people of whom it is inexact to say that they have an occupation or a job. They have a calling. These are the members of the Foreign Service. This permanent corps of officers is analogous to the officer corps of the uniformed services, but because its members do not wear uniforms, the outsider may not realize that they have taken what amounts to special vows. The people who make up the Foreign Service are in a position not quite like that of any other group of professional people in the country. They are civilians who live most of their lives under a quasi-military discipline. They must go where they are assigned. They live mainly in one another's company. They are subject to the orders of ambassadors, who can take charge of their lives—and whose wives can take charge of their wives—not only during office hours but outside them. And they are trained to a code of obedience; they may advise their superiors, but they are not asked to consent. Policy, it is their business to recognize, is ultimately made by elected officials; the career foreign servant is simply the craftsman who carries it out. Moreover, as if these were not special characteristics enough, the members of the Foreign Service are still further set apart. If they want to follow their calling, which is diplomacy, they almost inevitably have to work for the government of the United States. They don't have the options of most other people. They are professional people who possess highly uncommon experience and skills, but who have no choice of employers.

Thus the loyalties of members of the Foreign Service go out to one another. They have a common and unusual relation to the world and a common set of problems. They have to worry about the education of their children in foreign countries; about servants abroad and high prices in Washington; about the separation of families, the temperament of the ambassador's wife and orders that send them where they don't want to go. For some in the non-Foreign Service world they are too far out; for others too far in. They have been called cookie pushers *and* Communists, the architects of American globalism *and* the agents of foreign countries—and sometimes by one and the same man. For Joseph McCarthy, the Foreign Service was the almost perfect target. He found in its members precisely those human qualities that aroused his profoundest suspicion: urbanity, perspective, discipline, patience, adaptability to foreigners, dislike of publicity. Thus, to add to their sense of a shared calling, the members of the Foreign Service also have a sense of being misunderstood and persecuted, which enhances the Service's inner cohesion.

Accordingly, all the normal complications of working from a base of operations are intensified in the State Department. A Presidential appointee, like myself, is the instrument for translating the policies of an elected Administration into the actions of career officials. But these career officials have minds of their own, professional pride and an *esprit de corps.* They have seen Presidents come and go, and they have seen Presidents' appointees come and go faster. If they are going to look upon a new boss's ideas with the same enthusiasm that he does, he is going to have to do more than merely give orders. He is going to have to make his way into the network of loyalties that already exists or to turn these loyalties in his direction. This means an act of accommodation.

There is accommodation and accommodation. People have entered the State Department from the outside who have become more royalist than the king, and have taken positions opposed to any of the principles for which they previously stood. They have accommodated to the system by allowing it to swallow them whole. But these cases are deformed responses to a genuine necessity. In a bureaucracy that contains people with brains and consciences, an unspoken bargain binds a man at the top to his subordinates. If they are to be instruments of his will, he must, to some extent, be an instrument of theirs. If he wants them to carry out his ideas, he must listen seriously to what they have to say, and show at least an occasional capacity to change his mind. It is poets and military conquerors who have a simple conception of power as the successful exercise of one's will. That is what writing a poem or knocking down the walls of Jericho is like. But in a political or bureaucratic context a man works through others.

The process known as "the delegation of authority" is rarely what it seems to be on paper. On paper it is a device which permits the man at the top, who wants to accomplish ten different purposes, to concentrate on one or two and turn the others over to subordinates, who, again on paper, are supposed to do what he wants them to do. The theory is that they are he; it is his mantle they wear and his authority they carry. But these bearers of vicarious authority are, after all, individuals in their own right. They see the job in their own way and give it their own accent, and their principal cannot spend his days looking over their shoulders. And often, when they speak for their principal, they are challenged and have to come back to the source of their authority for a renewal of their mandate. He has to step in, bringing to bear his authority not only for his own ideas but for theirs. If they work for him, he must be loyal to them. A man with the ultimate authority in an organization kills the morale in it when he never lets others borrow on that authority.

Thus the power presented to you when you enter the government turns out to have a price tag. Your reach and influence are extended, but your policies lose some of their sharpness of definition. They become collective products. The policy that was "yours" when you entered becomes no longer your property but the organization's. That is success in government: people have changed their minds and their actions, and not just the rules in the rulebook. But this success also means that the policy for which you stand, whether it is better or worse than it was when it was yours alone, is not what you originally contemplated. Indeed, as I worked myself into my job, I found myself, on occasion, pleading at the White House or before Congressional committees for policies and programs about which I myself had a residue of doubt. I didn't support policies and programs I thought clearly mistaken, but I supported a number of whose worth my organization was more convinced than I, and to which I myself simply gave the benefit of the doubt. It is this transmutation of policy as it moves through a collectivity that makes government at once a powerful instrument and a blunt one. It belongs, not entirely but in the main, to team players, to bargainers, to the gregarious, to men who like to get together with other people more than they like to see ideas clean and neat.

This is why, if a country wants superior architectural design in its public buildings, or a successful program of public support for creative people in the sciences or the arts, it had better see to it that its government stands behind such endeavors but gets out of the middle of them. A better job can probably be done by people and organizations less encumbered than a government by the need to meld variegated loyalties together.

Certainly, I would not want to overdo the emphasis on the glories of the collective product.

Two or three weeks after I had taken office, I had a long discussion with one of the senior officers in the Bureau. We examined a problem that had long given CU trouble, discussed it back and forth, and, at the end, I outlined, with what I thought was his understanding and agreement, a new way of dealing with it. A few weeks later, I asked him to come in and report his progress. What had he done about the new policy?

He said, "I haven't done anything." His tone wasn't insubordinate. It was professional, sympathetic, the tone of a doctor to a patient.

"Why not?" I asked.

"It occurred to me after I left your office," he said, "that you hadn't thought through all the implications of what you were saying."

"That could be," I said. "I often miss the implications of my ideas. What was it that I missed?"

"Well, if we do it your way," he said, "it will change the complexion of what we've been doing."

I paused while I looked at him to see if he was pulling my leg. Then I pulled myself together and went ahead.

"That was the thought I had in mind," I said.

He looked at me to see if I was pulling his leg.

"But we've been doing it the other way for twenty years," he said.

"That," I said, "is in itself a reason for a new policy. In twenty years things have probably changed."

From his expression, I might have been telling him that the sun was going to come up in the west tomorrow. And as the conversation progressed, I saw that I was attacking more than a mere policy. I was attacking a creed, an organization's faith. In defending his views, he didn't say "I," he said "We." He meant all the people with whom he had worked through all the years, all the people who had developed the old policy and believed in it. Was I indifferent to everything that they had done and suffered? Was I saying that, for all that time, they had been wrong? Was I asking him to be disloyal to them? Indeed, I seemed to be asking him to do what nothing in his experience or in the experience of his colleagues had prepared them to do. I was really proposing a form of technological unemployment, and he wasn't so much refusing to do what I wanted as saying he couldn't do it. His reflexes didn't work that way.

This is the simplest source of the steady, unwitting resistance which new policy encounters in government. A new policy dispossesses people; it takes their property away. The point of what they know how to do, of what they have always done, is lost. The old outfit, the old group, loses its rationale, its importance, its internal pecking order. New people move into place; the established routines are disturbed. A change in policy seems somehow arrogant. Why should the legacy of the past, the wisdom of the group, be challenged? Why should things be thrown into confusion when they have been running so smoothly?

I recall an officer in the Department who was the government's specialist on an international agreement affecting tariffs on educational materials. The United States had signed the agreement, but, for sixteen years, had neglected to implement it by passing the legislation necessary to incorporate it into the tariff code. The officer of whom I speak had spent these years nourishing and guarding the agreement, answering people's questions about it and keeping the prospects for it alive. When I told him in my office one day that I had made a decision, with the earnest support of the White House, to push hard to get the agreement finally implemented, I had a nervous moment or two. The ends of his mouth twitched; he tried to form words but couldn't. And then he poured out all the reasons why people would oppose the agreement and all the difficulties we would encounter in trying to get it implemented. As success in what he had for so long been trying to do loomed over the horizon, this gentleman began to look increasingly like a man about to see his ancestral home torn down to make way for a new turnpike. He didn't quite believe what was happening; he understood the necessity but resented it; he was plainly worried about where he was going to live afterward. He had become accustomed to his place, alone with his agreement, suspended indefinitely between signature and final implementation.

When there are head-on collisions about policy in the government, this element of simple disbelief in change, of proprietary interest in the status quo, is almost always present. It usually comes to the surface in disguised form, and it exerts its greatest influence not in the form of active resistance to change but in the form of passive cooperation with it. For it is fortified by the procedures of government. What loyalty to the past doesn't do, the democracy of committees does. The normal way to treat a new idea is to "staff it out," to get a committee working on it. When the process is completed, the chances are overwhelming that the new idea will have been ground down into the old categories, the old habits of thought and action. The process is not a conscious one. The picture has not been painted gray by people who knew it was meant to be green. It is painted gray by people who see green as gray.

Despite the happy theory that policy-makers on the sixth and seventh floors of the State Department are in charge, policy has a tendency to percolate up from below. George Ball once told me about a conference he had had with a group of Department officers. He had told them what he thought American policy toward a particular country should be, and they had replied that he was wrong—the Department's policy was quite different. The Under Secretary of State repeated that, after having considered the arguments on all sides, he was telling them what policy should be. They continued to suggest that surely he was making a mistake. He was, it was intimated, getting too far out in front of—the phrase is always used—"the Department." The committees, over the years, had thought differently. And "policy" was what emerged from this laborious, persevering and depersonalized process. The suggestion that specific individuals make it had a touch of blasphemy about it.

"The Department" is always present, impalpable, vast, moving at its own speed, living on its own terms. Ideas must always be studied, cleared here, coordinated there. The product of that process is not likely to diverge sharply from what has been inherited. In most of the bureaus of the Department there is a feeling, created by the procedure of rotating people in and out of posts, which is characteristic of career services. The ship's officers come and go, the ship remains; and the function of the officer while he is aboard—one says, "Welcome aboard!" in the State Department to the new man coming in—is to stand watch and to see that the ship avoids collisions and stays in good repair. A man comes to an assignment, and he is told what policy is. He must find a way to navigate through the storms, to resist the pressures of people and events, and to turn over the policy to his successor in the same condition in which it was when he received it from his predecessor. Thus there tends to be an established tradition in each area of foreign policy, a doctrine accepted as a geographical fact is accepted—it is just there. Castro and Communism are the overhanging problems in the Latin American bureau; the Far Eastern Bureau has domino its theory.

As a result, the best thinking in the American government, the original thinking that leads to changes in action, is usually restricted to responses to crisis. Castro's victory in Cuba made it possible to think seriously about an Alliance for Progress. The missile crisis in 1962 started us in a serious way toward détente. The situation is not dissimilar in domestic affairs. It was the Russian sputnik that got the federal government seriously involved in American education.

The inertia of government, the sense within it that change is somehow unjust or impious, means that when alternatives to what exists are under consideration, they are usually narrowly conceived. The larger the change proposed, the heavier the case against it. This is one of the soundless causes of the drift of the American government into the Vietnam quagmire. In the end, after all the evidence was in, after the committees had done their work, the choices put before the President tended to be essentially limited choices, defined within the framework of accepted doctrines. When people have spent years trying to piece together a jigsaw puzzle, experimenting with this program or that, this government or that, this military expedient or that, they become committed to the proposition that the puzzle can be solved.

Thus "decision-making." All the time that policies are studied, choices defined and orders given, one can hear in the background the muffled sound of papers being shuffled to protect acquired positions, whether intellectual or bureaucratic. "Options are kept open," as the saying goes: the committees continue, the old offices remain in existence. And innovation, when it succeeds, tends to bear the marks of its birth in crisis.

6

The Politics of Consensus: Excerpts from a Log

October, 1965:

The secretariat of the Task Force is producing extremely good material, and the excitement of the people on it as they work their fifteen-hour days is contagious. It has already been transmitted, I think, to some of the other people in the Bureau. The people on the secretariat tell me they haven't had so much fun in years.

However, the secretariat is badly undermanned; nothing in the way of extra staff or money has been made available. This may be a straw in the wind. The word about the President's new initiatives in international education has still to reach the Bureau of the Budget, right there on White House soil. At any event, if the word has reached the Bureau, other words have too. There are rumblings that the budget now being prepared for submission to Congress in January will provide for a substantial reduction in the Department of State appropriation, and most particularly in CU's. I have urged people in the Department's budget office and at the Bureau of the Budget that the President cannot announce a bold new effort and at the same time reduce the programs that are the prototypes for this effort.

✷

The first meeting of the Task Force was held today. The meeting went well. I was particularly pleased at the fact that, although the government members of the Task Force are high-ranking officials, most came themselves instead of sending deputies. They seemed interested, even eager, although they threw in the necessary amounts of cautious skepticism.

In my own mind, I am taking the problems one at a time. We won't try the impossible, but within that very broad limit I think we should make the political decisions about what to present to Congress only after we've first decided, on independent grounds, what is really needed. Right now, the problem is to overcome the tribal suspicions of the executive agencies involved. HEW and AID are flexible and affirmative. USIA is a little surprised that we have come even this far and worried about where it all may lead. The Bureau of the Budget seems essentially puzzled: it's perplexed by discussion of international education outside the framework of technical development or promotion of the American image. And, of course, there really are some difficult administrative and policy problems in what we're discussing. Only if we can come up with reasonable and not too explosive solutions to these problems are we likely to overcome the doubts that exist.

The proposal for a new corps of Education Officers, made within the context of a broader proposal for new legislation in support of international education, has practical advantages. It avoids—let us hope—a head-on collision with USIA; it invites people to address the problems of international education from an educational point of view, which is precisely the point of view that is usually neglected; and it brings into the act a powerful department, HEW, where education is a central business, and not, as in USIA, AID or the State Department, an afterthought. HEW has the size and influence to give visibility to the idea of international educational cooperation. With John Gardner and Frank Keppel in the key spots there, I have all the more confidence in recommending that it be given a large responsibility for international education.

The best solution of all, I suppose, would be the creation of a new, semiautonomous agency, outside any of the existing departments, rather like the National Science Foundation. Its board of directors could come mainly from private life, and it could be responsible for all our long-range educational and cultural relations with other countries. Such an agency could focus on foreign affairs in a way that HEW cannot, and it would provide a smaller and less bureaucratic setting for cultural diplomacy. However, although I mentioned this possibility in the report I submitted in June, it would be foolish to try to get acceptance for it now. The ground isn't ready. The next best proposal, it seems to me, is to create Education Officers, and to give HEW larger responsibilities in international education.

❋

The President is making more and more noises about economy. The message has come to the Department that everyday expenditures are going to be reduced—official travel, office furnishings, overtime help, paper clips.

❋

The Task Force completed two days of meetings today. As a result of the discussion, I think we now have the language we need to explain why education should be moved front and center in foreign policy. We also have language that should prevent the interpretation that this is an effort to spread the American gospel. The members of the Task Force, particularly the private members, were vocal on this score. We are talking about mutual exchange, improvements in our own educational system and responding to requests that others make to us.

All the specific proposals for legislation or administrative reforms, with one exception, were approved in principle. The one exception on which we didn't agree was, as I had expected, the proposal to establish the corps of Education Officers in our embassies abroad. USIA's was the only dissent, but it was strong, even though we are not contemplating more than twenty to thirty such officers at this time.

*

The word reached me today that CU's budget request for next year has been reduced by more than 25 percent. I doubt that this can be the President's own decision. It doesn't square with the existence of the Task Force. I think I shall have to spread the word that the President has made commitments to international education in a public speech. The word hasn't gotten around. There are days when it seems that each part of this government conducts its business in a separate closet.

*

The suggestion has now been made—I am not sure whether it comes from our departmental budget office or from the Bureau of the Budget—that substantial savings could be achieved if we reduced our programs in Western Europe. The large flow of privately supported exchanges with Western Europe, it is argued, makes government programs unnecessary. I find this idea singularly unpersuasive. Private programs don't begin to be large enough, and this is no time, in any case, for this government to say that it is uninterested in cooperative exchanges with Europe. The Europeans are beginning to have doubts about us for enough other reasons. Besides, the binational commissions that administer the programs in Western European countries are, in effect, international educational foundations. They are the potential nuclei for all sorts of programs for educational, scientific and cultural cooperation. And European intellectual opinion still gives the principal lead to intellectual opinion around the world.

*

The President discussed our Task Force's affairs with a couple of his assistants the other day. He sent a message to me: "You're not going to make a program just for those Ph.D.'s, are you? I want to do something for that little boy at the end of the line who can't read or write."

As one of the President's assistants has told me, there is a difference in emphasis, and probably in fundamental philosophy, between the President's approach and mine. The President's interest in international education is the interest of a man who has known children who couldn't go to school. I am thinking mainly of the need to strengthen a community of intellect and imagination, and specifically of strengthening communication among the most highly educated people in the world. I'm by no means indifferent to the elimination of illiteracy, and I don't see any reason to make international education simply another gravy train for professors. But, in my own mind, intellectual community, simply in the nature of things, comes first. The United States won't be able to work successfully with other countries in the accomplishment of the kind of program President Johnson wants unless a pattern of confidence and understanding has first been established between American educators and their counterparts.

*

I had dinner with Barbara Ward, who was pleased to find me in the government. She looked at me as though I'd walked off with an oil well. "This President is like a great natural force," she said. "A Niagara of power. You have such opportunities. You can help use this power for the right things."

I said that I did feel as though I were plugged into a great source of power, but occasionally I felt the shock of a short circuit.

November, 1965:

I have been making loud noises about the proposed budget cut, and I was told today that the reduction may be only 15 percent. I accepted this news with the grace of a man being told that his house was not going to be blown up but merely burned down.

The pressure is severe on the budget people. They have received the word from the President that appropriation requests simply have to be slashed. The action in Vietnam is costing more, I gather, than anyone originally thought it would. Yet I think the President means it when he speaks of a new international education program or of other education and welfare measures. It seems to me that the President genuinely wants economies *and* a "Great Society"; he wants to fight a war in Vietnam *and* to build dams and democracy in the Mekong Valley. He hopes all these things are simultaneously possible.

Still, down here where I sit, the effect is disconcerting. On Mondays, Wednesdays and Fridays, we receive messages to go full speed ahead; on Tuesdays, Thursdays and Saturdays, we're told that we're going to have to retrench. This may be the politics of consensus, but it feels more like the politics of the swinging door. The door opens, and when you start to go through, it slams in your face.

✻

The Task Force began its final two-day session today. There were fireworks about the Education Officer proposal, but we made progress on most of the other proposals. The most important is the recommendation for an International Education Act, which will provide a program of long-term support to colleges and universities.

＊

This was the last day of the Task Force exercise. I came to my office around 7 A.M. and wrote a new statement on Education Officers that would offer a compromise. In essence, it would allow the Education Officers to review all educational proposals submitted abroad by the Information Agency or any other section of an embassy, but it would leave Cultural Affairs Officers with most of their direct responsibilities for operation of exchange programs intact. The Education Officer, in contrast, would be a planner and coordinator—something that many ambassadors have said they needed, and something I certainly need in my position as chief coordinating officer in the government for international education programs. It is hard to do that job in Washington without having an agent in the field to translate decisions into actions.

I wasn't sure that I should propose such a compromise, since there was only one negative vote against the original proposition. The Task Force would obviously like the Education Officers to take over the educational exchange programs entirely. But it's not going to be possible to change to such a system at once: after all, we haven't even begun to recruit Education Officers, and they are not going to be easy to find. I don't see the point in creating a major disturbance when we couldn't put the decision we took into effect immediately in any case. Besides, the program the Task Force is designing is large and ambitious. It has many parts to it, and will need the cooperation of people all over the government. It would be a mistake to leave a trail of blood behind, just to win one point absolutely. The compromise version preserves the basic principle: it puts a man concerned with education next to the ambassador, and keeps him out of the chain of command of agencies with other primary missions, like AID or USIA.

I presented this new proposal to the Task Force and ran into trouble from both sides. The USIA still wouldn't take it, and most of the others preferred the stronger proposition of the day before. The compromise was finally adopted, however, although the one dissenting vote remained.

✳

The secretariat has been putting the report of the Task Force in shape, and it has been a breakneck affair. But I have had successful meetings with heads of other agencies and the President's advisers, and we have achieved, I think, not only a meeting of minds but some measured enthusiasm about the new plans.

The Secretary of State is in Latin America at a conference. I sent a copy of the report to him for his signature and received a long telegram from him. He had taken his editor's pencil out and had gone to work. The report is the better for it.

✳

The report is at the White House, now signed by everyone, including USIA, and I have been attending talks with representatives of the Bureau of the Budget. John Gardner, Frank Keppel and others have also been involved. The Bureau's people obviously don't know where the money's coming from.

December, 1965:

The White House Conference on International Cooperation has made a strong report on education and cultural affairs, much in the same vein as that of the Task Force, and calling particularly for the separation of educational and cultural programs from propaganda. The urgent tone of the report is probably more important, however, than its details. It should help the Smithsonian initiatives.

*

The ice finally appears to have been broken so far as the proposal to cut the CU budget is concerned. I prepared a memorandum, and George Ball came back from a meeting with the President to predict better weather. I am told that the budget cut for CU will be only 5 percent, which is about par for everybody this year, or perhaps even a little better. Having gone through quite a boxing match over this budget, I now feel as though I've won a victory. And if the International Education Act and other Task Force proposals go through, the total expenditure for international education will be materially higher.

*

There are bureaucratic complications arising about the status of the Education Officers. The original thought, way back last summer, was that they would be HEW officers, chosen in co-operation with State, and, naturally, under State Department authority when overseas. But there has been too much trouble in the past with Agricultural Attachés and others, who act like independent agents in many places overseas. So I have willingly gone along with the Department and the Bureau of the Budget in supporting the idea that the new Education Officers should be unequivocally members of the Foreign Service. Among other things, this should make it easier to put them into embassies without adding to the glut of people already assigned overseas. An Education Officer could replace a Foreign Service Officer doing other, less urgent functions. And some Foreign Service people, of course, would be excellent Education Officers.

The arrangement will continue to be a cooperative one with HEW, which will share in the recruitment, selection and training of these officers. HEW apparently will also be able to provide, within its budgetary request, for the financing of this new corps. This will allow the two matters that are intertwined

—the International Education Act and the Education Officers—
to be considered together by the same elements of the Administration and by the same Congressional Appropriations
Committees.

All of this has been remarkably easy to work out. Both John
Gardner and Frank Keppel are quick and flexible, and they
couldn't care less who does what, or who gets the credit for it,
so long as it's done and done well. I sense, however, that some
of the people further down the line, in their Department and in
mine, are going to look inside every comma of the agreements
between us to be sure no one's bureaucratic property has been
given away.

*

My life grows more complex.

Just to sum up, among other things, I have been working on
English-language teaching abroad, the Russian exchange agreement, the use of surplus currencies in Tunisia, a possible India-
U.S. educational foundation, the forthcoming meeting of the
Cultural Council of the Organization of American States, to
which I will be the chief delegate, and the approaching official
conference with the Japanese on cultural cooperation, pursuant
to the Kennedy-Ikeda agreement. What are known in the Department as "everyday problems" also keep me occupied. An
"everyday problem" is one which could be solved in ten minutes
were it not for the fact that somebody somewhere has decided
that the fate of the world depends upon it. This requires longer
meetings and keeps more people occupied.

Meanwhile, the international education program is gradually
taking shape. Money, of course, is the problem. Vietnam's
costs keep rising, and people are also beginning to talk about
inflationary pressures. I ventured the informal opinion at a
meeting today, at which some economists were present, that,
in view of these pressures, perhaps the time had come for a tax
increase. They looked at me as if I needed my head examined.

Not that they argued on economic grounds. The proposal, they thought, was politically impossible.

❋

The Senate Foreign Relations Committee apparently intends to conduct public hearings on Vietnam. Not many people in the Department or the White House like the idea. My own view is that it may move the subject back into the realm of public debate, which would be much better for the country.

❋

The new international education program may or may not turn out to be new. The money is going to be found, at least at the beginning, essentially by reallocating the funds within existing programs. The Agency for International Development will spend more money for education and less for other things. Other agencies will alter priorities. And some new money, we hope, will come to HEW, through the proposed International Education Act, but it will not be much at first.

I don't find myself too concerned about the money in itself at this point. The program will take time to launch, and money shouldn't be spent in more than modest amounts before other countries have given tangible indications of their desire to join with us. But we have to give tangible indications of seriousness of purpose, and allocation of money is one way to do it. Moreover, when money is merely reallocated within agencies, there is always the risk that the bureaucrats down the line will simply make paper changes, redefining what they're doing in a new vocabulary but not necessarily doing anything really new.

Still, notwithstanding these reservations, I'm persuaded that we've made progress. The spotlight has been focused on international education, and the President's authority now lies behind a new view of the importance of educational cooperation and cultural exchange.

❋

The bombing pause has begun, and we've got people traveling through foreign capitals looking for openings that may lead to negotiations. I'm not sure I understand how this kind of highly publicized diplomacy can work, but the bombing pause is good news, and who knows? A man on Capitol Hill said to me today: "Johnson's a magician. I think he may bring this off."

January, 1966:

The President's Address to Congress on the State of the Union contained an immense number of legislative requests. He has done much more than affirm that we can have both guns and butter: if he's right, we can have guns, butter, détente, civil rights, civil harmony, better education, better cities, price stability and fundamental Constitutional changes—for example, extending the term of Representatives to four years. The message is impressive for its energy and for the imaginativeness of many of the ideas it contains. But in its boundlessness will it merely leave people feeling weary or skeptical?

※

On instructions from the President, one of the President's assistants and I paid a call on Senator Fulbright, and asked him whether he would sponsor the International Education Act in the Senate. The Senator listened with care, expressed his sympathy with the Act's purposes, but replied that he thought it would be better to treat the bill as domestic legislation, since it provides only for grants to American colleges and universities and would be mainly administered by HEW. The Senator thought that if he managed the bill, it would probably be treated as legislation mainly in the field of foreign affairs. While his committee should have an ancillary interest in the legislation, it should not be the principal committee concerned with it.

In consequence, the Administration will probably turn to Wayne Morse, who is on the Education Committee.

*

According to some of the newspapers and weeklies, an effort is being made to bring about a thaw in the relations between Senator Fulbright and the President. One of the reasons for this view, it surprised me to learn, is that my name was spotted on the Senator's list of visitors. I am in the Administration, and he was involved in my appointment: the conclusion is that I must be a go-between. The assumption that is not made is that I was there on a straightforward piece of business. So far as I know, however, that was my errand. The President made a businesslike proposal to the Senator, and the Senator replied in the same spirit. Neither an overture nor a rebuff—simply two men doing their jobs.

*

We have been working on the President's forthcoming message on international education. The basic decisions, and almost the exact language, have all been firmly established.

*

I addressed the Cultural Council of the OAS today. The meeting is heavy on panoply, but I don't think the Council takes itself seriously. My references to the President's Smithsonian Address did manage, however, to stir some hopeful reactions.

*

The Senate Foreign Relations Committee began its hearings on Vietnam today. They kept Secretary Rusk at the table for six or seven hours. Fulbright and Morse were particularly sharp, but most of the other members were in on the action. The Secretary held his ground. He's durable and disciplined:

the session was on television, and though he's a chain-smoker, he didn't smoke during the entire session.

✳

I am in Honolulu for a meeting of the National Review Board of the East-West Center, which is part of my jurisdiction. Honolulu is paying a lot of attention to this meeting; the East-West Center is important to it. There is also much hopeful speculation about the implications for the Center of the President's international education program. So there have been lots of headlines about my visit. The headlines right next to them are about the Rusk-Fulbright confrontation in Washington.

February, 1966:

The message on international education and international health was sent to the Congress today. It refers to William James's "moral equivalent of war," and says in part: "Education lies at the heart of every nation's hopes and purposes. It must be at the heart of our international relations. . . . We expect to receive as much as we give, to learn as well as to teach."

The message then goes on and lists eighteen separate actions. The third has to do with Education Officers. The President proposes to "create a Corps of Education Officers to serve in the United States Foreign Service." "As education's representatives abroad," says the President, "they will give sharper direction to our programs. Recruited from the ranks of outstanding educators, they will report directly to the ambassador when serving in foreign missions."

Not many people will know the acrimony and the hours that went into the decision to include that brief and disarming phrase, "report directly to the ambassador." It is the phrase which pulls the Education Officer out of the USIA chain of command.

I took part in the press briefing at the White House concerning the message. The reporters took it very coolly—no hard news or immediate sensations in it. The question that interested them most seemed to me to come from out in the bleachers: Was the Administration planning to spend money on birth-control education?

※

The President is in Honolulu, meeting with Marshal Ky. The bombing has resumed.

7

The Better-Informed
Government Official

I used to imagine, when the government took actions I
found inexplicable, that it had information I didn't have. But
after I had served in the government for some months, I found
that the issue was more complex: often the government does
know something that people on the outside don't, but it's something that isn't so.

People worked hard to keep me informed during my days
in Washington. The reports, analyses, clippings, evaluations,
cables, fell on my desk as snow falls in a blizzard. But after a
while I came to suspect that I might not be dealing with hard
facts, but rather with a world created out of hunch, hope and
collective illusions.

I think it was the case of the folk singers in the boondocks
that brought this suspicion to a focus. The case came to my
attention about three or four months after I took office. One of
CU's most effective programs, I had been told, was its sponsorship of tours by American folk singers, who went out into the
boondocks to entertain Indian peasants or African villagers. So
I asked my colleagues in CU who were responsible for the

program to tell me about it. What did they mean when they called the program "effective"? And what was the evidence of this "effectiveness"?

It took my colleagues a little time to convince themselves that I really wanted to know, but they finally settled down to explain the obvious to me. The folk singers, they told me, were vigorous, youthful, clean-cut and gregarious. They went out into the villages and the bush, where other Americans rarely went, carrying their guitars and singing, joking and dancing with the natives. A rousing time was had by all. That was what they meant by calling the program "effective."

But how did we in Washington know that this was so? I asked.

At this point I received an answer I had come to recognize: I had received it many times before with respect to other questions. We knew from "reports from the field."

But could this not be due to the fact, I asked, that the officers in the field who wrote the reports liked folk singers and enjoyed a little Stateside entertainment?

No, my colleagues answered me, these officers in the field reported that the villagers liked the folk singers too.

But how did they know? I persisted. Had they conducted opinion polls? And even if they assumed that the reports were accurate, what difference did it make? Why did Indian peasants or African villagers have to like American folk singers? What was gained? What were the objectives we were trying to accomplish? Or were we being diverted from asking this basic question by the pleasant sound of a little laughter and applause?

I have to report that a note of modulated impatience came into my colleagues' voices. I seemed to be missing the obvious point: if peasants liked American folk singers, they would like America. But I persisted: even if these evenings of folk song ended with everyone's joining in a chorus of "The Star-Spangled Banner," would not these raptures fade? Would the effects of an evening spent listening to songs in a strange language really last very long? And if the memory did last, would the villagers farm more efficiently, or vote better, or even take more pleasure in music?

Pressed to the wall, my colleagues brought out their big guns. Did I not realize, they asked, that the Russians were trying to win these people over into their camp?

I rejected this reply as nonresponsive.

But President Johnson himself, they said, had noticed the work of one of these groups and had invited its members to the White House, where he had poured praise on them.

At this point, I realized that I had tracked the quarry down: folk singers were "effective" because they called the President's attention to CU's program and CU could use that kind of support. As a test of the effectiveness of a government policy, it seemed to me equivalent to testing the effectiveness of a surgical operation by taking the surgeon's blood pressure after the operation's completion. We had begun by looking for evidence of the effectiveness of the program in India and Africa. We had ended by finding that it was effective at the White House.

I still have an open mind about folk singers. What I learned from this experience, in fact, was that after years of experience with such a program, and after reams of paper had been covered with words, the government could supply me with next to no substantial information calculated to make my mind less than wide-open on the subject. And I think I also grasped a lesson of wider import from this experience. The system for providing information that supports the sending of folk singers to the boondocks bears fundamental similarities to the system for providing information that supports the government's sending engineers to the boondocks, or soldiers. It is a system with a bias toward self-deception built into it.

Large-scale government is an effort to solve an ancient metaphysical problem—the problem of action at a distance.

The condition of having to act at a distance has a relation to government, and particularly to foreign policy, rather like the relation that sex has to human life. It is a commonplace fact, the existence of which is known to everybody, and yet it is a source of some of government's deepest mysteries and most intractable problems.

A man launches an action on the bureaucratic sea. But he is never there, where the action comes to shore and where people have to live with its consequences. The report of what he has done must travel back to him across thousands of miles and past scores of people. And the problem is aggravated by the elusiveness of the standards by which people in government judge their success or failure. The man at the top of a large business organization, though he may be far away from the oil wells or the salesman's counter, sees results in growth charts or in profit-and-loss sheets. In government the criteria of success are shakier, the outcome sought more diffuse, the domain of relevant facts less neatly defined.

Throughout the American government there goes on a constant search for "evidence of the effectiveness" of policies. One has to give an answer to this question almost every day to the Bureau of the Budget, Congressional committees or the press. But what *is* evidence? And what does "effectiveness" mean? Is the success of a community-action program to be measured by statistical increases in average income? By more votes for the Administration at the next election? By the reduction of militance in the ghettos? By the increase of such militance? And what is the span of time within which we are making these judgments—one year, two years, five years? The rules of the game aren't clear. As in the Irish game of hurling, you play the ball, the man and the feathers.

Under the circumstances, a facile equation is always in danger of taking over: a "good result" is a "good report," and a "good report" is a report that is approved by somebody whose approval counts. Standards of judgment are adopted not because they are relevant but because they are convenient. Government officials begin to act like the drunk who, having dropped his wallet in the Bronx, went down to Forty-second Street to look for it because the light was better there.

What are the factors that make for distortion, and that have to be guarded against, in the government's information-gathering process? The first is an institutionalized tendency to look on the bright side of things.

One of the functions of the government's reporting system is to provide the people at the top with what they need to defend their policies against attack. The American system of government is an adversary system; it is surrounded by an adversary press; and in the world at large an ideological struggle is going on in which the American government is a major target. The members of an Administration are not going to be helped, when they go before an Appropriations Committee, or when the Administration to which they belong goes before the electorate, if the information with which they are armed reports that their policies are a tissue of errors.

I recall numberless meetings in the Department of State to discuss emergencies that had arisen. I recall very few in which we did not spend time reviewing the record so that we could show hostile critics that the Department had been doing what it should. To some extent, of course, this is necessary. A government cannot govern without making an effort to explain and defend itself. But one of the dangers is that the people most effectively persuaded will be the members of the government itself. George Romney was wrong to say that he was brainwashed by American officials in Vietnam. In all probability, those who did the "brainwashing" were merely trying to make him see things as they themselves did.

But even if we didn't have an adversary system of government, the government's reporting system would probably contain a danger of self-deception. The physicist Heisenberg is famous for the so-called "principle of indeterminacy." It holds, not to put too fine a point on it, that, in the subatomic world, when you look for a fact the mere act of looking changes that fact. There is room for a dissertation on the Heisenberg Effect in government. During my first months as Assistant Secretary I asked for information about our policies with regard to a number of subjects in a number of countries. My inquiries duly disappeared into the channels of communication within the Department and out to embassies halfway around the world. In the course of time, the answers came back. To my surprise, a large proportion stated that inherited policies were "under review," and that whatever it was that the Department had been doing, it was trying not to do it again. Merely in the effort to inform myself, I had apparently produced changes in policy. Somehow, I had emanated skepticism and a desire for reform; I had got back the emanation that there were no foot-draggers in the field.

Inside the government there is not only a flow back and forth of facts and judgments; there is also an exchange of emanations. The man at the top sends out a query. He may think that all he wants is the cold facts. But along with his question he also conveys an attitude, a set of hopes and expectations. And the man at the end of the line who receives the query, though he may think that he is reporting only objective facts, is usually reacting as well to the emanation he has received. And so he emanates back that he is hard at work, and that he understands and believes in the boss's policies. The chances are slim that he will send back a report that things aren't working, for such a report is susceptible to only two interpretations: either the boss's policies are wrong or the man on the spot is incompetent. The man on the spot does not have to have been around very long to know which of these interpretations the people upstairs will choose. Killing the messenger who brings the bad news is an old custom.

Thus there is a kind of propitiatory optimism that creeps into government reports. To be sure, many sharp and hard-hitting reports do come in. On the whole, however, they are outnumbered by those which season objective reporting with the sugar of positive thinking. And this tendency is reinforced by the fact that reports go back through channels, and that people all the way along the line read them. A man can guess the reactions if he takes a negative tone: What is he trying to do? Destroy morale? Hurt the organization? Such concerns may be only half-conscious, but they affect what people in government say to each other. "Keep the faith, baby!" is an unspoken injunction.

Indeed, it sometimes creates a faith that would not have existed without it. At each stage along the line of command, the man who has to write a report or execute a policy sees only part of the whole picture. From where he sits the policy may seem unintelligible. But other people are carrying it out, and other people appear to believe in it. So a kind of rolling commitment to policy is created. At each stage, the responsible person imagines that somebody up the line has looked at the policy in cool objectivity and has seen that it is good. He writes his report in that faith and thus passes the faith along. And each man further along passes it to the next until it reaches the top man, who absorbs the faith, assuming that, since everybody else has it, there must be something to it. And so, though nobody is lying, everybody may be deceived. Thus, in government, "truth" is always in danger of collapsing into St. Paul's definition of faith: the evidence of things unseen, the substance of things hoped for.

A second source of distortion in the government's information system is the influence of short-range bureaucratic considerations. Broadly speaking, the material in government reports falls into two categories. The first consists of broad studies of the questions at issue and projections of trends that are two, three, five or ten years away. The second is short-range: it tells about events as they unfold, deals in personalities, describes shifts of power or opinion that may or may not be permanent, reports the progress of negotiations. As a day-to-day matter, the first kind of report does not compete successfully with the second for most government officials' attention. For no matter how much sound study goes into the long-range reports, they are shots in the dark. History is too full of contingencies, politics too full of accidents, for a practical official to bet heavily on long-range speculations. What is real, what is indubitable, is what is here and now—General De Gaulle's intransigence, Mayor Daley's anger at a recent federal action, this month's wave of strikes. The light is clearer where these events are, and so one focuses upon them.

Besides, the very nature of government forces this point of view upon an official. Despite all the money that a government spends on research and analysis, its major job is operational. In foreign policy, certainly, most officials enmeshed in operations do not have the time to think two or three years ahead. They may assent to the abstract proposition that "peaceful engagement" should replace the cold war; but what does that tell them to do specifically about the new traffic restrictions imposed on the road to Berlin? And in domestic affairs, too, this is frequently the case. Officials can say, and believe with all their hearts, that "law and order" without concern for social justice is an inadequate approach to riots in the slums; but what does this have to do with a decision to send the National Guard, tonight, into Detroit?

Indeed, at the end of a day spent in making decisions of this sort, the official may well wonder why he should spend the evening reading the scholarly treatise on the future which arrived on his desk in the morning. Is long-term policy created by abstract theorizing about future goals? Or is it created out of the succession of immediate, practical decisions of the kind he has been making all day long? The life of an official does not merely turn him aside from more spacious reflections; it creates in him professional habits and a kind of professional pride which lead him to believe that reality is where the nitty-gritty is, that policy isn't made by the great thinkers but by the tough men who take each problem as it comes and do the best they can with it.

Normally, therefore, long-range projections of policy have only a cautionary function for the man with operational responsibilities. They warn him against certain kinds of action. He should not be too bellicose with the Russians. He should not use force unrestrainedly. But these inferences from long-range principles do not tell him how to disengage himself from the present, as it is, so that he can move under his own steam into the future. The decision-maker may take an hour or two off from his work, attend a meeting where a long-range report is discussed, and stretch his mind a bit. But he then goes back to his office to answer the phones.

Moreover, long-range reports have trouble competing with the short-range reports for another reason. The latter is the kind that deals with "crises." I do not mean crises like the discovery of missiles in Cuba or a threat of war over Cyprus, but crises like the approaching visit of a loquacious Congressman to Paris, or the publication of a story in the newspapers about American students in Madrid picketing the American Embassy. The majority of the "crises" with which short-range reports deal are of this second kind. They are not events which, considered in themselves, are likely to have a profound or enduring impact. They are important only if the final judgment on what the official is doing will be made tomorrow. Unfortunately, however, the official usually has to live as though there were only tomorrow. Congressional appropriations are voted each year. In this time frame small things tend to bulk large.

Moreover, officials are pushed into focusing on small things by the newspapers, which thrive on exposé and revelation, by members of Congress who need the opportunity to nit-pick in order to show the people at home that they are on the job, and by the scores of hangers-on, in every department, on the staffs of Congressional committees, in the corridors of the White

House, who justify their presence and their salaries by looking worried over small events, and by turning them into big problems which they can then busy themselves solving. In every field, and in foreign policy especially, the essence of the high official's task is to separate the superficial crises from the genuine ones, and to keep the former in their place. But keeping minor crises from being inflated beyond their just proportions is a major task. Riding in an automobile with a Cabinet officer one day, caught in a traffic jam that was making us late to an important meeting on an unimportant matter, he turned to me and said, "I think I can take almost all of this job—the hours, the abuse, the damned foolishness. What wears me out is trying to mollify all these eager people who love fires."

Edward Gibbon remarked that in understanding history there are two kinds of facts: the everyday facts of individual actions and the large, commanding facts which give a pattern to events and govern their evolution. It is this second kind of fact that tends to be submerged in the day-to-day operations of the government. Attacked for the condition of the cities, officials of the Johnson Administration regularly replied: Hasn't there been Head Start, and Vista, and a new Department of Housing and Urban Development? The sense that the total national effort gave such disproportionate attention to other things as to make these measures look like token contributions to the collection plate on Sunday did not show in what they said. Beleaguered on all sides, officials involved in Vietnam policy took comfort from the number of hamlets secured, or the statistics of people reached by Revolutionary Development teams, and argued in hurt tones that their critics were unaware of the progress being made. But what was on their critics' minds was a kind of question with which the flood of short-range, bureaucratic reports did not deal: for example, if the United States government is still perceived as an alien, meddlesome presence in large parts of Mississippi or Alabama, why should its representatives be expected to have a quick and profound impact, except negatively, in Vietnam? This is the kind of question that busy men in government, immersed in their work, are likely to ignore. And they are helped to ignore it by the paper curtain the government puts between them and the outside world.

Moreover, what comes to be accepted as the truth in government is usually a combination of factual and political judgments. This is a third source of distortion in the information system. The government's reporting system has a large element of bargaining in it, even though the bargains aren't usually explicit. Through its communication system a government builds a politically viable view of reality, a body of acceptable ideas on the basis of which an effective coalition of power and interest can be created. What is taken to be true, therefore, is often what it is politically desirable to believe—an act of accommodation that has also been known to take place in individuals' lives and even in universities. When the reports of the CIA's intrusions into academic and youth activities in the United States and other countries became public, I was struck by the stubbornly optimistic judgments about the consequences which came to Washington in reports from the field, and which officials in Washington eagerly seized and accepted. The majority opinion was clearly that the effects would pass, that people elsewhere were sophisticated enough to understand that all governments did this sort of thing, and that the reputation of the United States had not been seriously damaged. I was thoroughly convinced that these soothing notions were false, but I also think I know why people held them. The CIA is powerful; its judgments cannot be dismissed; its judgments, therefore, have a prima-facie quality of truth about them.

When an official receives an appraisal of a situation, he does not look only at what it says. He also has to take account of who says it and who else will read it. The standards by which he should judge the report's accuracy may be equivocal, but one kind of fact is always close and clear: this is the political "clout" that a report carries. The process of transmitting and evaluating information inside a government thus has an uneliminable political ingredient. A communication is an event in a system of power and authority. It may come from a man whom it would be trouble to replace, or from an organization with which you are trying to work out a program of cooperation; it may come speaking for a powerful and troublesome constituency, or express only the views of an isolated individual working without support. These considerations are taken into account, consciously or unconsciously, in deciding what shall be accepted or rejected as the official view of reality.

Not that the independent facts are neglected. Judging from my own experience, the higher one goes in the government, the less the discussion of an issue turns off into a discussion of its politics. I recall one meeting in 1967 related to the Arab-Israeli conflict, at which a young staff assistant, proud of his political realism, alluded to the fact that the Administration was not entirely free to judge the issues on their merits because of the "Jewish vote." The remark was treated as a sorry exercise in junior-executive Machiavellianism. He was simply told, by some of the highest officials in the government, to focus on the facts of blockade, freedom of passage and United Nations commitments. On the whole, in government meetings people talk about the evidence and not about what it would be convenient or prudent to believe. But the evidence, naturally enough, is accepted or rejected in terms of men's unexpressed notions of what is "credible"; and in government, as in most other domains, "credibility" is affected by what people are able to believe, willing to believe and find it supportive to their egos to believe.

At every government conference table there is always, in addition, the element of rank, hierarchy, power. It depends very much on who is chairman of the meeting whether people will talk frankly or the argument will be cut off before it gets going. And the outcome of the argument also depends, usually, on who is who at the table. George Ball lost repeated arguments about Vietnam between 1962 and 1966 not because he lacked powers of persuasion, but because he was bucking powerful tides of policy moving in the opposite direction, because it was easier to make a small decision to escalate than a big decision to quit the game, and, not least, because he was an Under Secretary, arguing against Cabinet members and the heads of a vast military establishment. It is easier for a President to bet that an Under Secretary is wrong: the President pays less of a price for doing so.

Is this so very different from life in other domains? I don't really think so. But the massiveness of the government's machinery, and the way in which the noises this machinery makes envelop the people working inside it, increase the severity of the problem. Only those who are constantly aware of the nature of this machinery, and of its dangers as well as its uses, can protect themselves against it. This is particularly necessary for the people at the top of the bureaucratic pyramid. There is a special function of leadership in government, over and above the articulation of policy, decisiveness in crises or the ability to pull disparate groups together. This is to clear the air, to introduce an element of saving skepticism into the government's communication system. The men at the top communicate by emanation. They can emanate respect for candor, impatience with clichés, a desire to know, or they can emanate the message that the function of the system is to salve their wounds and fan their fevered brows. Which they do has an enormous effect on the government's grasp of realities.

The attitude they take toward "the experts" is also important —particularly in foreign policy. "Expertise" in this domain does not consist in mastery of a science with an elaborate structure of confirmed laws. It consists in a combination of close knowledge of the facts mixed with intuitive judgments, and, not infrequently, with the sentimental attachments to an area which a professional student of an area is likely to develop. (I recall a conversation with one of the nation's leading students of Southeast Asia, at the time that the Arab-Israeli conflict was coming to a head. He said to me, in the tone one uses to state the obvious, that, of course, Southeast Asia was more important to the long-range interest in world peace than the Middle East. I reflected that most experts, no matter what their subject, thought that subject more important than others.) But even apart from the special bias which they may bring to a subject, the specialists often sustain the premises of existing policies without intending to do so.

For what is it the expert usually does? He is assigned a specific task; he is told to produce a *specialized* report, written within a pre-established frame of reference. It is not the specialist's official business to pass judgment on this frame of reference, and few specialists do. If they have been asked to propose remedies for the balance-of-payments problem, they do not point out that the problem would largely disappear if the country had smaller military commitments around the world. They take these commitments as their points of departure and come up with remedies, if they can, within that context. They leave "more general questions," as they say, to higher authority. But higher authority is busy, distracted, harassed; and, almost always, it is committed up to its ears to its major premises by the decisions it has taken in the past. It naturally resists engaging in a review of its first principles, and it is fortified in this resistance by the specialists' reports it receives. Vast amounts of knowledge and brain power have gone into them; they represent the expenditure of untold man-hours, effort and money; there is an investment in them. And they have usually accepted the basic premises of existing policy; at any rate, they have raised no questions about them.

Thus the nonspecialist who dissents when higher authorities meet is swimming upstream. He can say that, despite reports from the field, he believes that the revelations about the CIA's intrusions have had a much more serious impact abroad than the reports suggest. He can say that, despite all the careful analyses of the progress of "nation-building" in Vietnam, he expects that nationalism is growing in the country as a reaction against the American presence. But what can he produce to support these suspicions? Only his own judgment of how human beings are likely to react, only what he thinks is common sense. Against him are the briefcases crammed with reports, the stacks of papers on the table, the graphs on the wall—the visible products of much money, much work, much faith. It might be extremely salutary if the writers of specialized reports were not permitted to hide themselves inside their expertise but were required to say what they think, as men as well as experts, about the basic premises of policy.

Undoubtedly, Congressional fact-finding committees some-times serve the function of providing the government with another perspective, but the executive probably needs its own instruments of self-criticism as well. The Constitutional system of checks and balances pushes Congressional committees, as often as not, into an adversary role. Reacting to their attack, the executive branch takes up its position on the other side of the courtroom. And after it has made its defense, it tends to be more strongly committed to its policies than before, for the rhetoric it has employed to state its case has become more inflated, and the reasons for what it is doing have come to seem more important to it. It can thus talk itself into intransigency. The executive needs its own monitor. That is why, setting aside the more flamboyant cloak-and-dagger aspects of the CIA, the original idea of creating a service for gathering and evaluating information, independent of the armed forces and the Depart-ment of State, was a sound one. Operational responsibilites en-courage self-serving reports. Unfortunately, however, the CIA was promptly given operational as well as reporting responsi-bilities, and so the idea was spoiled.

At the very least, the man at the top of an operating agency needs staff people around him who have no operational ax to grind and who have been given their assignment because they are not believers. The requirements of efficiency in government have to be weighed against the requirement for protection against too much consensual thinking. Tidy tables of organization are instruments by which a top administrator makes his life more "efficient" by arranging to be systematically uninformed or deceived. When information and advice flow upward through ever-narrowing channels, the paneling on the walls and the rugs on the floor of his office do not save the man at the top from living in an isolation cell.

The phenomenon of self-deception in government is not a passing problem, like a broken leg. It is a permanent condition, like the body's tendency to go flabby without exercise. Shortly after I left the government, I read a newspaper account of an interview with Commander Herbert L. Ogier, who had been captain of the destroyer *Maddox* in the Tonkin Gulf incident in 1964. In this interview, Commander Ogier told about his growing doubt that the *Maddox* had been the object of a sustained torpedo attack from North Vietnamese naval units. Two of the reports that torpedoes had been launched were perhaps authentic, but nineteen subsequent reports, in Commander Ogier's words, may have "resulted from our putting our rudder over, you see, and this was reflecting the sound of our own screws up toward our sonar. . . ." The Commander concluded, "I felt like I'd more or less been tricked or something by myself."

I didn't know about these doubts of Commander Ogier's while I was Assistant Secretary of State. But looking back on my government service, I wonder how much of what government hears is really the sound of its own screws, reflecting off its own rudder and coming up through its own highly selective sonar.

8

The Artificial City

If the government often seems strangely deaf to messages from the outside, its information system isn't the only reason. Life in the government of the United States is a special kind of life because it is life in Washington.

The Founding Fathers invented Washington. They were thoughtful men, and one must suppose that they knew what they were doing, but it is difficult to think so. They wanted a capital that would have no ties to any state, and the result was an artificial city, constructed on a site that had been shunned as a place of urban habitation during the hundred and fifty years in which settlers had roamed up and down the Atlantic seaboard looking for places to live. The Founding Fathers wanted a city that would belong neither to the North nor to the South. They got what they wanted, and we still have it—a capital too far north to escape the snows, and too far south ever to be prepared for them, a neutral, in-between place, of mixed styles and uncertain tastes, where the magnolias bloom in the slush. Washington, as John Kennedy said, is a city of Southern efficiency and Northern charm.

Yet Washington has, of course, a distinctive flavor. It is, to begin with, two cities, not one. The larger city is composed of people who have fled to a federal enclave in the hope of escaping poverty, degradation and the aftermath of slavery. The other and smaller city—Washington Northwest and its suburban appendages—is inhabited by a ruling minority most of whom think of someplace else as home. Like the rulers of Taiwan, their eyes are on a continent over which they claim authority, and they have only a tangential interest in the place where they reside. And in this Washington a culture, a way of life, prevails unlike that of any other major city I know. Alone among the great capitals of the world, Washington—Washington Northwest—is a one-business town. Every view in it is a political view, and practically every avenue to success is an avenue through government.

Even Washington's everyday language is the language of a segregated community. People speak, as unaffectedly as though they were speaking English, of GS Twelves, FS Threes, NASMS, Wristonization, Memcons; they refer to "flaps" (public controversies), "crunches" (head-on conflicts), "arm-twisting" (persuasion), "knocking heads" (reaching an agreement).

What catches the newcomer's attention—at any rate, what caught mine—is the city's surface discipline and orderliness. Strangely, it possesses a quality that can only be called serenity. In Washington's offices the papers move through channels, and in the streets the automobiles seem to move through channels too. The traffic runs on one-way roads toward the federal office buildings in the mornings; in the evenings, along the same roads, the traffic flows one way in the opposite direction. No doubt my memory deceives me, but the deception is itself significant: I don't recall a single incident of tailgating, a single angry argument between drivers, during all the time I drove or was driven through the streets of Washington Northwest.

I don't even recall anyone's ever trying to push through a door ahead of me in Washington. On the contrary, the man ahead of me usually held the door open for me. I speak literally, of course, and not metaphorically: in government, getting through the door first is half the game. Still, a recollection of unruffled decorum is a striking one to take away from two and a half years of life in a city of a million people, and an American city at that. It was when I journeyed outside the city, to New York or Cleveland or New Orleans, that I had a sense that American society was a precarious arrangement; on the streets of Rome or Paris I saw and heard more to remind me of Vietnam than I did on the streets of Washington.

All this, of course, has changed. The march on the Pentagon in the fall of 1967 was the first large breach in the walls of Washington's enclosure. The fires in Washington, after Martin Luther King's death, carried the process much further. And even before these events, of course, Washington was a place whose side streets and parks were dangerous, a place where there was anger and hopelessness. But it retained on its surface—and, more than most other places, it still retains—what used to be called an academic atmosphere. The telephones ring, the cables pour in, yet a riot in Detroit or a war in the Middle East keeps a distant, hypothetical quality. The ceremonial rounds and the cocktail parties continue; the directives and the carefully prepared announcements issue forth; the gossip goes on, the names changing but the stories essentially repeating themselves. Washington generates the feeling that the eternal verities are secure: commotions come and go, but in the end the Congress will be droning on, the Civil Service will be assigning each man his place in the great system, the Washington Monument and the Lincoln Memorial will still be in place. Like monastics, the inhabitants of Washington Northwest aren't easily distracted, for they live in the Light that flows from the True Center.

I never quite got over my surprise at the curtain of ceremony and protocol that comes down even around an Assistant Secretary of State. I don't suppose that people feared that I would wander off the reservation, but I was rarely allowed outside alone. When I went to a meeting in another building or to a hearing on Capitol Hill, I was accompanied by retainers. They opened the right-hand door of the car for me, I entered and settled back in my seat, and then one aide would sit next to the driver, and the other would hurry around the car and come in at the left. I struggled for a while against this system just as I struggled against the public-passive voice in government prose. The outcome was about the same. I succumbed, managing only to save a few remnants of principle. For example, no matter how quick or dexterous my aides were in reaching for my briefcase, I always held on to it firmly.

Even this much independence caused me trouble. On an official visit to Yugoslavia I was accompanied by one of my friends and colleagues in CU. On the flight we managed to forget about Washington and protocol, but when we landed and the Yugoslav protocol officer came aboard the plane to usher me out, my friend's reflexes reasserted themselves. It was a warm day, and he reached for my hat and coat to carry them. I pulled them away from him, saying that I was perfectly capable of carrying them myself. Frustrated, he reached for my briefcase. We emerged from the plane and stood at the top of the stairs, each of us clutching the briefcase and trying to pull it away from the other. I surrendered only because I saw the TV cameras grinding away and had to step forward to shake the hand of the Deputy Foreign Minister.

The capital of our egalitarian country is a rank-conscious city. In most cities people perceive a man, of course, in terms of his position, but in Washington people go out of their way to keep him from forgetting who he is. A man's rank isn't only registered in the décor of his office or the pictures on its walls. It is registered in the place he is assigned at the dinner table and the obligations that go with it. If he is the ranking guest, people wait to go home until he leaves. Twice during my first

months in Washington, I sat irritably, as the hour fled past
11:00 and 11:15, waiting for somebody to break the spell and
leave so that I could decently follow suit. On each occasion I
finally managed to gather from my wife's mysterious signals that
everybody was waiting for me. I knew I was acculturated when
I came to grasp the finer nuances of leave-taking: 11:00 is about
right; 11:10 shows you have been having a ravishing time;
11:15 suggests that you've forgotten who you are and what you
represent.

Thus it usually does no good to take an official out for an
airing. He gets no airing at all. His job comes with him. Even
if he isn't thinking of what he is saying—and he had better be
—others are thinking of what they are saying to him. The lady
who interrupts a conversation you are having about the balance
of trade with someone from the Treasury, and bursts into an
enchanting description of her visit to Kenya, turns out to be
making a pitch for Kenya as against Somaliland. The man who
starts his conversation with you by quoting Aristotle on education turns out to have an experimental program for the education of teen-agers which he thinks the government ought to
support. And across the room your wife, to whom you look to
bring you news from the world of free spirits, is listening, with
that fixed expression you recognize, to an official of the Information Agency. The gentleman is telling her that foreign lan-
guages are overrated, and that Americans have no need to speak
any language but English, even those Americans in foreign
service.

"What did you say?" you ask your wife on the way home.

"Nothing," she replies. "I thought you already had enough
philosophical disagreements with the Information Agency."

For a man—or his wife—isn't seriously committed to the
business of government if he is prepared to disagree with people just for the pleasure of speaking his mind. The art of politics consists in not making enemies unintentionally. And so
the imperatives of the government committee meeting or the

diplomatic negotiating table take over in Washington's drawing rooms. A man's position gets in the way of relaxed communication with him in many walks of life, but in Washington his official position is like a wart on his nose: it is the thing that seizes attention, and he can't separate himself from it except by a form of surgery. The freedom in anonymity that men can find in other cities is hard to come by in Washington. With whom, then, does a high official put up his feet and talk? Who will tell him, irreverently enough to get his attention, that he is spinning wheels uselessly or has fallen into a policy that makes no sense? To the insulating effects of the government's internal communications system are added the insulating effects of organized social life in Washington.

Not that the American talent for creative disorder doesn't break through. It broke through noticeably even during formal visits to the White House.

One evening my wife and I attended a state dinner in honor of the President of Pakistan. It was our first such experience, and on the way to the White House I reminded my wife of the movies we used to see in the thirties about court life in prerevolutionary Russia. "Do you remember," I asked, "the man in the great tall hat, standing at the top of the stairs, announcing, 'The Duke and Duchess of Samarkand,' and then the slow, stately descent down the stairs while all the rest of the guests watched? Are you all set? That's what's in store for us."

My wife wasn't in a mood to be amused. She had just acquired reading glasses and wasn't adjusted to them, and she was worried that she wouldn't be able to see her name on the seating list. "I can't ask some Marine guard to read to me, can I?" she asked.

It turned out, to our surprise, that both of us were on the target. After we had taken off our coats, a handsome Marine immediately took Helen in tow. I trotted obediently behind while he escorted her to a table where the lists were laid out, found her seating card and read it to her, without her asking. The White House was prepared. And then we were escorted down the hall to the entrance to the East Room, where another Marine, standing at attention, announced us to the assembled guests. "The Honorable and Mrs. Charles Frankel," he called out, using good republican language for the peerage, and I entered with my wife, wondering whether the Duke and Duchess of Samarkand had ever performed their roles better. We stood around, and, after a while, there was a fanfare, massed flags appeared at the entrance to the room, and the two Presidents entered. We were presented to them in order of rank and went in to dinner.

It was then, as I learned later from Helen, that creative disorder intervened. There was an empty chair at Helen's table. During the fish course a stocky gentleman, in dinner jacket like the rest of us but with cowboy boots on his feet, wandered into the room and deposited himself in the chair. He was feeling pretty good, having taken a wee drop or two, and he began by giving his attention to the décolletage of the lady next to him, which he apparently found both astonishing and pleasing. After she fended him off, he turned his attention in the other direction and noticed he was at the table next to the President's. He leaned back, waving to the President, who didn't notice him, so he leaned back still farther, still trying to catch the President's eye, and broke the back of his chair. The situation was handled well. A couple of the gentlemen with watchful eyes who were standing about the room picked him up the moment he touched the floor, and inserted a new chair beneath him.

Then the steak arrived, and the gentleman, whose dinner companions were now eagerly encouraging him to take some food, set to and attacked it. But he had found the White House chairs too flimsy, and he now found the White House knives too dull. So he reached into his pocket, pulled out a hunting knife, opened it, cut his steak, wiped the blade on the tablecloth and put the knife back in his pocket.

All told, he went through three chairs, and by the end of the dinner the Secret Service was providing extra service at Helen's table. Later on, despite this surveillance, our hero walked into a waiter who was carrying a tray full of coffee and liqueurs, producing a satisfying crash of bottles, cups and glasses. At that point, the gentleman disappeared from view, and slapstick more or less disappeared from the evening's entertainment.

But not all White House humor is slapstick. Some is subtle social commentary. At another dinner, this time in honor of the King and Queen of Thailand, the President, the King and their ladies entered after the usual fanfare, followed by violinists who took up positions around the room. They struck up a tune, and then, in solemn order of rank, the assembled dignitaries—Cabinet members, Supreme Court Justices, Senators, *grande dame* Alice Roosevelt Longworth—paraded past the chiefs of state to be received. The tune to which we marched was "Never on Sunday."

I don't think anyone else noticed. Form dominates content in the White House, as in most other places in Washington.

Looking back, however, I think that perhaps the most broadening result of my exposure to Washington was my education in the meaning of culture. As Assistant Secretary for Cultural Affairs, I had an opportunity to do research in "culture" which has been vouchsafed to only a few. It may be helpful to the anthropologists, philosophers and many others who have argued about culture to record the fact that in Washington, the center of power in the world, there are four principal definitions of the word.

Definition Number One is probably the most popular. It is illustrated in sentences like "He spends his evenings in cultural pursuits" or "He went to the Cultural Center." "Culture," in this definition, stands for the performing arts. The novel doesn't quite fit—not if *Lolita* is a novel. And neither does poetry, which is usually produced and enjoyed in private, and requires an active effort from the reader as well as the writer before it can be enjoyed. "Culture," in the public, political sense of the word, requires celebrities, crowded places, opening nights and ample intermissions.

I was the only Secretary of any kind in Washington with the word "Culture" in his title. It had its pleasant side. I could go backstage whenever I wished and meet ballet dancers. But Congressmen who had spent ruined evenings at concerts their wives had made them attend were a little suspicious of me, and I often had the impression, in my meetings with hard-headed bureaucrats and administrators, that they felt a certain initial hesitation about talking to me about money or politics for fear that such talk might wound my sensibilities.

However, it was the lovers of Culture who gave me my greatest trouble—or perhaps it was I who troubled them. Somehow, I was not the man they hoped to find: my tastes were a bit too catholic. I like Ray Bolger as well as Paul Taylor, Zero Mostel as much as Olivier, and there was music written after Wagner which, apparently, I could tolerate. In fact, I had difficulty tolerating Wagner. In a survey I once conducted surreptitiously during an intermission at Constitution Hall—I recorded its results on the back of an envelope—I was able to determine that 2.56 of every 4 people in Washington who love Culture (Definition One) expect it to be refined and up-lifting. This gives them, these days, a restricted field in which to roam. Deplorable language is used on the stage; ballet is too explicit; music upsets the digestion. Culture in its basic sense has been reduced, for most of them, to "Swan Lake"—and not all of that. Besides, "Swan Lake" belongs to the Russians, which limits its usefulness in American foreign policy. In Washington, caught between the Culture haters and the Culture lovers, an Assistant Secretary of State for Cultural Affairs walks a thin line.

The second definition of "culture" that prevails in Washington produced problems too. I usually encountered it among economists and technicians. They used the word "culture" as in "cultural lag." Culture (not to equivocate) is what is wrong with the world. Why hasn't foreign assistance worked out in Country X? Answer: Country X's culture is an obstacle. Why doesn't a multinational organization like the United Nations Educational, Scientific and Cultural Organization achieve all the purposes that had been hoped? Answer: cultural differences. Why, despite the brilliant performance of the American economy, are there still people who complain about it and say that it turns out too many useless and ugly things? Answer: cultural prejudices.

The practical consequences of this view of culture were somewhat unsettling. If an Assistant Secretary for Cultural Affairs says that it is important to promote "cultural exchanges," he is likely to be interpreted as proposing an exchange of vices between nations. He is perceived as a brake on the wheels of progress, a man concerned with the traditional and the outmoded. One of the difficulties of my job, during working hours and afterward, was that the word "culture" set up all sorts of reverberations—the humanities against the sciences, books and other useless things against technical progress, the soft side of life against the realities of power, money and politics. There was always a latent question whether I belonged in a serious meeting.

Washington's third definition of culture is achieved by dividing Definition One by Definition Two, as follows:

$$\frac{\text{Culture: Performing Arts}}{\text{Culture: The Dead Hand of the Past}}$$

Knowledge of the new mathematics is not required to work out the quotient: "Culture" equals the dead arts, the monuments of times gone by. It is the nonperforming, noncontroversial side of a country—Williamsburg, the Temple of Abu Simbel, Canterbury, Chartres, Venice, the paintings of Picasso in the United States (but not his opinions), the opinions of Picasso in the Soviet Union (but not his paintings). "Culture," in a word, is a subject that offers a common ground to people who would otherwise disagree.

This definition of culture was by all odds the easiest for me to live with. So conceived, "culture" gave me a unique function to perform in Washington's foreign policy community: as Assistant Secretary of State for Cultural Affairs, I was the man who was kept around to change the subject whenever things got hot. This definition of "culture" permitted me to live with the handicaps of my position and to carve out a niche for myself just the same. Still, I confess that I was a little restive under this definition of my role. I couldn't quite manage to stand for nothing but neutrality. "Are you still sending that dancer, Josie Lemon, abroad?" a Congressman once asked me, and I had to confess that if it wasn't José Limon it was probably another dancer named Alvin Ailey. "My God, who?" he asked.

I ran into difficulties with the Russians too. They have reasons, philosophical and political, for preferring the idea of culture as something inert. The Russians once turned down an American candidate for the exchange program who proposed to study contemporary Moscow dialect. When they were asked why, they said that they could not provide him with facilities to do his research. Translated, this meant that his research would require him to walk around the streets and talk to living people, which, under the Russian definition, would not be cultural exchange but cultural penetration. This example may suggest why, although I wanted to do my bit to dispel the clouds of the cold war, I sometimes had disagreements with my Russian colleagues. I found it hard to subscribe to a definition of culture which reduced it to the customshouse definition of an antique: something that can be imported duty-free because it is purely decorative and is more than a hundred years old.

My view of culture as active was the subject of a conversation between a Russian diplomat and myself. The United States and Soviet governments were in the midst of negotiating the renewal of the cultural exchange agreement, and the negotiation wasn't going well. The Russians blamed it on the war in Vietnam, which they said had created a bad atmosphere for negotiation. At a reception in a neutral embassy, I ran into the Russian cultural attaché, a cheerful, vigorous man with whom I had agreeable relations. I said to him that I hoped he realized, and would tell his Ambassador, that there were no political obstacles on the American side to the conclusion of a new agreement.

He replied: "Mr. Secretary, I am happy to have this reaffirmation of intentions from your side, and will tell my Ambassador. But you are a philosopher and you should know that culture is a frail flower; its health depends on the soil in which it is planted, and that soil is the soil of politics. The soil now, I am sorry to say, is not good. It has turned—how do you say? —sour."

Thus did the representative of one great superpower speak. And I, the representative of the other, replied: "No, culture is not a frail flower. Culture is a busy bee. It flies from flower to flower, and in the process fertilizes the plants and enriches the soil. Culture can change politics."

"One can see, Mr. Secretary," said the attaché, "that you are not a Marxist, not a materialist. You believe that culture can change the base, that the superstructure can affect the foundation."

"Yes," I said, "I do. And on this point I am in full agreement with Engels, who said that Marx and he weren't so foolish as to imagine that ideas had no influence."

"It is unfair of the Americans," said the attaché, smiling, "to appoint a professor of philosophy to their government."

The agreement was in time signed. Unhappily—or perhaps happily—nowhere in it, as I recall, is there a formal agreement on the definition of culture.

It was the fourth definition of "culture" which I ran across in Washington that had the greatest possibilities. In this definition, "culture" stands for anything that takes people away from government, politics, business or anything organized. These are formal and impersonal. Culture, in contrast, is informal and personal. "Cultural relations" means "people-to-people" relations—and diplomats, businessmen or officials, it goes without saying, are not people.

There is something to be said for this point of view, I suppose. At any rate, a good deal was said in favor of it in my hearing in Washington. I met some enthusiasts for this definition of culture, however, who rather startled me. One evening, after a dinner at the house of one of Washington's patrons of the arts, I was buttonholed by an advocate of the people-to-people technique in international affairs. He urged me to propose a massive exchange of persons with the Russians: we would send ten of our best colleges and universities—students, faculties, families and all—and install them in permanent enclaves in the Soviet Union, where they would pursue their normal American activities. The Russians would do the same thing to or for us, sending their best people and institutions of learning. Through such people-to-people exchanges, the gentleman argued, each side would be deterred from dropping bombs on the other. After absorbing this thought for a moment, I intimated to my companion that he was proposing an exchange of hostages and not what was normally meant by an exchange of persons. He looked at me with disappointment and mumbled something about the conservatism of the State Department. But by that time I was already beginning to play with the idea. If we could send some people I knew, and if the Russians sent us some of theirs, and if we could just arrange to let the trade stand . . . But I didn't let him in on my thinking. In Washington you have to play your cards close to your vest.

Washington's conceptions of "culture" suggest something else about the city. Its preoccupation with politics, its overwhelming professionalism about government, give to politics and governmental affairs an air of abstractness. The British government in London, the French government in Paris, the Italian government in Rome, are governments on which an alien and external world intrudes, tougher, larger, more durable than they are. They are surrounded by people who are indifferent to their existence or hostile toward it, by buildings, neighborhoods, traditions, institutions, that speak of other days and other regimes. In Washington the American government has nothing to push against except itself. In consequence, it lives in danger of a kind of political solopsism. Lyndon Johnson, who offered Ho Chi Minh an irrigation project as a token of good will, who looked out on the nation and the world as though they could be managed in the way he had managed the Senate, is a product *par excellence* of Washington.

In no other important city of my acquaintance, except perhaps Moscow, is a single view of what is normal in human behavior so predominant. In Washington, Everett Dirksen is unique, but he is not regarded as unconventional. Like Marilyn Monroe, he merely carries a particular convention to the peak of perfection. In contrast, Dr. Spock is perceived as passing strange: in the world of professional politicians and career government officials, the traditions of the Abolitionists or the Quakers are half-forgotten stories read in children's books. The mores of a society are revealed in the eccentrics it takes in stride. Washington takes in stride the eccentric who can find a place for himself within the American two-party system. If it has a soft place in its heart for the idea of rebellion, it is the kind of rebellion that has a tradition and the memory of a government behind it: the old Confederacy is the model.

Thus Washington is separated from the United States twice over: once because it is so predominantly a political city and twice because that makes its politics distinctive. The politics of Washington is more self-enclosed, more stylized, more provincial in its illusion that politics is all there is.

At its center stand two special human types—the professional politician and the permanent government official. The professional in politics is set off from the amateur precisely because they both occupy the same terrain. The professional deals with issues that are everybody's business, but he deals with so many of them, and deals with them so steadily, that few of them have the ultimate, soul-saving importance for him that they do for the amateurs who are interested in them. Most amateurs enter the political process because some particular matter has become important to them. Politics is for them a means to an end, and what counts is to gain that end. To the professional, in contrast, what counts is to endure. More likely than not, he has causes to which he is attached and principles in which he believes. But he lives in an arena where many causes and principles collide, and he usually recognizes, therefore, that he cannot expect to win each point. On the contrary, the path of wisdom is to avoid betting his all on any single issue.

Thus a certain dissonance affects the process of communication between politicians and others. Even when there is agreement, the tone of voice, the sense of commitment, are at different levels. Indeed, the very realism of the politician's code make it, at moments of serious trouble, unrealistic. The ordinary bread-and-butter politician is liable to stumble when faced by an issue, like Vietnam or civil rights, around which moral passions have arisen. He finds his instinct to deal and bargain thwarted. And so he often tends to resent the existence of such issues and to be suspicious of the people who raise them. And because the professional politician today—and particularly the senior, well-entrenched politician—may spend as much as ten or eleven months in Washington, shut up very largely with people of his own kind, this dissonance between the professional and the amateur is accentuated. There is a tendency for politicians to be surprised by the existence of people who don't play their game.

Thus, when deeply divisive issues arise, a kind of curtain comes down between the political professional and the political amateur. A minority of politicians have the capacity to speak and hear through this curtain. The majority is screened off. What the political amateurs hear from them, above and beyond what they may or may not say, is a tone of voice that seems inappropriate to the desperateness of the issue being discussed. And what the professionals hear from the political amateurs is a shrillness and impatience that set off their defensive reflexes. In Washington the usual antiwar demonstration, far from making its point, has an opposite effect. It is not the opposition to the war that seizes the politicians' attention, but the demonstration's unconcern for the rules, its attitudes of intransigence and self-righteousness. The demonstration thus tends merely to reinforce the politicians' sense that they are in the presence of a danger to their way of life. And so they meet intransigence and self-righteousness with an intransigence and self-righteousness of their own. This is not good for communication between members of the politicians' guild and nonmembers. It is particularly bad for communication between politicians and the grievously discontented.

Moreover, in setting Washington's tone the politician is helped by that other principal denizen of the city, the permanent government servant. He, too, lives by an unusual code. Assuming that the government for which he works is a constitutional one, a permanent official's conscience must not bleed when he is asked to carry out a policy that doesn't fit his own ideas. Indeed, he requires a conscience which tells him, except in extreme circumstances, to pipe down after he has had his say, and to get to work in support even of what he thinks is wrong. For the electorate hasn't bet on his political opinions or conscience. The only bet it has made, and for which it has paid its taxes, is on his professional integrity and competence. A citizen who scoffs at the men who live by this code doesn't know his self-interest. A democratic regime is in trouble if its "permanent government" is composed of people who look on official policy, no matter what it is, as an effulgence of divine infallibility. But it also is in trouble if its permanent government is insubordinate, or if it is made up of people so partisan in their political views that they leave the government whenever it isn't to their liking.

And yet, admirable though this code is, long and conscientious allegiance to it exacts a price. After a while a man's sympathies go out more spontaneously to the good soldier than to the brave rebel. And with the trappings and authority of government all around the official, this tropism is strengthened. A man is working for the nation; the flag is at his side. Why should unruly people on the sidelines make the nation's problems more difficult? It isn't true that the federal government is filled with people who are merely putting in their time. On the contrary, most government servants, and particularly those in the higher ranks, work with a sense of commitment which can be found, I suspect, in few businesses, factories or universities. They are in the government because they think the government is doing important things, and they find their work significant and exciting. The result, however, is that they don't live in the same mental and emotional territory as the discontented or the alienated. And they lose the sense that the code appropriate to a permanent official isn't necessarily a code appropriate to everyone else.

The day before I was scheduled to leave office, a month after my resignation had been announced, an old acquaintance of mine, whom I had known in my graduate student days, came to say good-bye. He had spent his life in the State Department. "What was the matter?" he asked. "Couldn't you stand the heat?" No, it wasn't that, I replied; I had rather enjoyed the heat. I had simply found it time to leave a government which, for all the good things it was attempting to do, seemed to me very wrong about the two or three biggest issues it faced. Certainly, in my own area of responsibility it was going backward not forward; I could not, by my presence, give support to this. "It's what I said," he replied. "You can't stand the heat. Few outsiders can."

This is the pride of the guild member, and it isn't special to the American bureaucracy. The officials of most governments have the same feeling about keeping up the public appearances, the same respect for fidelity through thick and thin. But this professional spirit is fortified and hardened, in Washington, by the circumstance that officials meet too many of their own kind and too few of any other. In consequence, they move from obedience to their own moral code to the attitude that no other moral code is respectable.

The pervasiveness of this attitude goes far to explain, I think, why the government tunes so many disagreeable noises out. People in the permanent government are not consciously unwilling to listen. But they prize discipline and teamwork, and every inclination in them tells them that some people and some ideas are out of bounds. I don't recall encountering a single official in the State Department who questioned the right of any citizen to sign petitions or demonstrate against the war in Vietnam. But I knew a number of officers who felt, as by a kind of conditioned reflex, that people who made trouble for their government at a difficult time weren't responsible people. They couldn't listen to the opinions of such people with seriousness. They turned themselves off, by an act of only half-conscious volition.

The American government's method of dealing with dissent is not the crude or unscrupulous method which the more militant or innocent of its critics imagine. In the executive and legislative branches there are some people, of course, who are not averse to punishing those who disagree with them. It would be surprising if such people weren't around: they are around in banks, churches, unions and universities, and their political hue ranges from red to red-white-and-blue. But most people in government are more sophisticated, and they take the Con-

stitution seriously. The American government's method of dealing with dissent is quieter and more gentlemanly. It doesn't
involve the conscious suppression of dissent. It involves, on
the part of countless good government officials, simply the
unconscious tendency to discount dissent, and particularly
the kind of dissent that can't be called "constructive." The
dominant mores of Washington proclaim that usable dissent,
the kind of dissent worth listening to, is the dissent that goes
through proper channels.

Do people in Washington never break through these conventions? On the contrary, no one can doubt, after living in
that city and encountering the obstacles to communication that
exist there, that the desire of human beings to communicate
is unconquerable. In a car in the middle of a traffic jam, at
night on the corner of a terrace, some of the highest officials
of the government confided their doubts to me, and then went
back to do their work in the cause they doubted. As the Vietnam
war mounted in intensity, it was eerie to discover the number
of Cabinet members and top military men who doubted or
disagreed.

Washington is not a cold or impersonal city. The friendships
one makes there have a special warmth, rather like the friendships one makes in military service. Nor is Washington entirely
without resources—a few Senators, occasional itinerant scholars
with nothing to sell, some temporary officials not yet house-
broken—that help it to step back from itself and adjust its
sights on the world. And if the members of the press never
wrote a line, most of them would earn their pay. They are
the government's other communication system. Without them
information and debate would fall, even more than at present,
within the boundaries prescribed by the White House and
Capitol Hill. But the gentlemen of the press, on the whole,
have the standing in Washington of Muslims or Jews in a
medieval Christian city. It is recognized that they perform

certain unavoidable functions and have to be tolerated. But it is also recognized that they remain unconverted and may, at any moment, be dangerous.

The city lacks a sufficiently large and self-sustaining life of its own apart from politics. It has too many people who are enlisted, committed, working for something practical, working for somebody important. It has too few active but detached minds. It remains, indeed, pretty much what the Founding Fathers intended it to be—a neutral meeting ground. Like Geneva, Panmunjom or the Church of the Nativity at Bethlehem, it is a place of odd contrasts and precarious compromises, over which there hangs an unspoken taboo against any decisive or original action that may break an unstable truce.

Washington has a beautiful setting and an atrocious climate, broad vistas and small-town gentility. It has as fine a collection of first-rate minds as can be found in the United States, but lacks a first-rate secular university. It is a place where big money is made, but it is not a center of commerce and industry. It is filled with monuments to the achievements of the past, but has trouble keeping a theater going. And while it is remarkable for its collections of works of art, any collection of artists usually embarrasses it. Its social life is elegant, and its conversation runs the gamut from A for Appropriations to W for Welfare, as in Health, Education and. . . .

Thus it is, I think, that the American government can go in for performances which sometimes suggest that its members are living under a collective spell. In January, 1968, after a summer of rioting and burning, after an ugly march on the Pentagon and a year of widespread civil disobedience, the President of the United States, in his State of the Union Address, took notice of the existence of such phenomena by referring to "a spirit of questioning" in the land. In Chicago in the summer of 1968, the Democratic Party, four years after it had pledged "no wider war," chose as its convention slogan, out of all the slogans available, "Promises made . . . promises kept."

Such performances can be put on only by people who have blacked out a significant portion of the external world.

Washington does for the American government what royal pomp, class barriers or censorship do for other governments. It muffles the sounds of disbelief and discontent. Only the Decline and Fall of the Johnson Administration has made it possible to say of the capital city of the United States that it has come to know—to know by direct, indelible acquaintance— just what kind of shape the country is in. It was the last to know, and it still gives signs that it is the first to forget.

9

*Eight Times Around
the Mulberry Bush:
Excerpts from a Log*

February, 1966:

Had a talk with Congressman John Brademas, who is managing the International Education Act in the House. He sees the Act, as I do, as incorporating a new formula for the federal funding of higher education. It is not a bill to provide manpower or meet an emergency, but to provide general funds to encourage educational change and experimentation while leaving the freedom to make educational decisions to the universities.

The Act, despite its name, provides exclusively for support to American institutions of learning, and we agreed that the proper approach to the legislative campaign is to stress that fact. The Act will authorize the expenditure, over a three-year period, of $140 million—not a very great amount, but a substantial improvement over the present. We share the feeling that the bill can be presented in a noncontroversial manner. If we don't turn the campaign for it into a crusade that promises too much and arouses people's resistance, we ought to be able to get it through.

※

The proposal for Education Officers is running into trouble. The Bureau of the Budget has expressed doubts that they should be funded from the HEW budget, since the main job of this new corps will be in embassies abroad. If BOB persists in this view, the prospects of the Education Officer program are considerably reduced. The past record of the Subcommittee on Appropriations for State suggests that it isn't likely to vote the necessary funds, small though they are. Just as much to the point, the Education Officer program is part of an entire new thrust in international education in which HEW plays a crucial role. The proposal for Education Officers can be best appraised by the committees of the Congress directly concerned with HEW and the International Education Act.

※

I saw Senator Wayne Morse today, to discuss his sponsorship of the International Education Act in the Senate. It took some time to get to the subject. He wanted to talk about Vietnam. He said that he expected forty or fifty Democrats to lose their seats in the fall elections. As far as he was concerned, he hoped that every man who supported the war would be beaten. "There isn't any other issue before the country," he said. When I managed to turn his attention to the International Education Act, he launched into a denunciation of the CIA, and said that he would want every kind of guarantee, before he supported the Act, that it was not an instrument for giving the CIA—or the State Department—any kind of power over American universities.

"Senator," I said to him, "we've had contacts in the past, even before I was in the government, and I think you know my views on such matters. I wouldn't be involved in this bill if I thought it had such an intention behind it."

"I know you," he said, "and I'm not saying anything about you. But I don't trust the crowd you're associating with these days."

He asked me a large number of questions about the bill, and said he was going to put his staff to work on more. Before he makes up his mind, he says, he's going to give me and my staff lots of homework.

✻

The change in the Congressional mood in the six months I have been here is remarkable. It doesn't do much good now, and it can often do harm, to say that the President is personally interested in a piece of legislation. Yet this is the same Eighty-Ninth Congress which, in its first session, was so compliant to the President's will. I was in the office of a Democratic Congressman today—he is a hawk on Vietnam—along with one of the President's assistants. The President's man remarked that he hoped the Congressman would change his mind about opposing one of the President's recommendations: if it were beaten, he said, it would be a "rebuff" to the President.

"It's time for a few rebuffs," the Congressman shouted. "Things have changed up here. You people downtown have twisted too many arms, and we're tired of it. The old days are over, and don't forget it."

✻

If somebody wanted to know what individual is most on the State Department's mind when it makes its decisions, and decided to find out by counting the number of times different individuals' names are mentioned during Department discussions, I hazard the guess that the answer wouldn't be De Gaulle, Kosygin, Mao or Ho Chi Minh. Next to LBJ, it would be John Rooney, Congressman from Brooklyn and chairman of the Subcommittee on Appropriations for the Department of

State. There is a trial by ordeal that Assistant Secretaries of
State must pass before they are really members of the club—
their first appearance before Mr. Rooney's committee. I had
my trial today.

As I sat in the anteroom awaiting my turn, I reflected that
the Founding Fathers had had their way. Undeniably, we have a
system of checks and balances. At any rate, we have the checks;
I'm not sure about the balance. The Congress and the executive
are separate, adversary branches of government. I watched the
witnesses ahead of me from the Department droop into the
hearing room when they were called. They looked like con-
victs going before a parole board. They wore the expressions
of men who were humble and eager to learn, and who were
appearing before their judges not to make excuses but to
demonstrate their desire to rehabilitate themselves. And when
I myself entered the room, trying not to look that humble but
not to look defiant either, I saw that Mr. Rooney plays his
own role to the hilt. His manner, his physical posture, his
look of impatience and disbelief, are those of a prosecuting
attorney—which is what he was before he became a Congressman.

I had hardly taken my seat when he asked me how I could
possibly justify a "grandiose" exchange program, which had
been going on for twenty years and was supposed to be winning us friends. All around the world, he said accusingly,
students and professors were demonstrating against the United
States. The reply came immediately to my mind: "Mr. Chairman, your committee also passes on the budget for the FBI.
Each year the FBI comes before you and tells you it needs
more money because the crime rate is rising. And each year
you take that as a perfect argument for voting funds to them."
But I didn't make this reply: it was another of the sacrifices
that I have had to make in public service, for it costs money
to score a debating point in a Congressional hearing. I restricted myself to saying that demonstrations against the
United States were part of the general political climate in the

world, and that our program had neither the purpose nor the capacity, by itself, to change people's reactions to the policies of the United States government. The cultural program had a different object: to keep the United States in useful, cooperative contact with other nations whatever the political frictions that might arise.

Mr. Rooney didn't listen. I don't mean that he heard me but was unpersuaded. I mean that after he asked a question he would turn to his staff assistants and talk to them while I was giving my answer. The question was from him to me; the answer was from me to the stenographer. It was all merely for the record—which he edits.

On the whole, he held his fire so far as I was concerned. His most biting remarks were directed at members of my staff, whom he knew from previous years. I have been warned that the next time around he will treat me like a recidivist too.

After lunch we went back before the committee to go over the budget for the East-West Center in Honolulu. The atmosphere was different. Mr. Rooney described the program as a product of his and LBJ's initiative, with an assist from Frank Bow, the ranking minority member of his committee. So he likes the Center. And perhaps his favorable attitude also comes from the fact that the Center is a physical, visible fact. The money isn't going into intangibles but into concrete.

Mr. Rooney's subcommittee holds its hearings behind closed doors. Without outside observers the proceedings have a star-chamber quality.

❋

I left for Japan today, to attend the Japan–United States Cultural Conference.

March, 1966:

The conference is proceeding well, but the two most important problems we confront are not on the official agenda.

The first is that these conferences have little continuing effect once they've ended. The second is the Japanese feeling that the era of American tutelage of Japan is over, and that our cultural relations must not be a façade for continuing the tutelary relationship.

Ambassador Reischauer and I agree with the Japanese. But agreeing with them, unhappily, doesn't solve the problem. The Japanese remain touchy on this point, which is only to be expected, and expressions of understanding from the Ambassador and me don't change certain facts that justify their touchiness. Many of the permanent officials in our embassy and Information Service retain, without realizing that they do, the attitudes and habits of earlier days. One man, for example, speaks of our obligation to repair "the information gap" from which the Japanese allegedly suffer—a nation that reads more books and newspapers, probably, than any other nation in the world! We need a new and younger group of men here. And it isn't only American officials who display such attitudes. A number of American professors, some of them rather distinguished, have come here and lectured as though it were necessary to introduce the members of this sophisticated culture to elementary truths.

*

The Japanese have accepted the proposal that a continuation committee be established, following this conference, which will meet regularly, and promote specific programs of joint study and research. However, the Japanese want the Japanese and the Americans formed into two separate but cooperating committees, rather than into a single joint committee. Our delegation saw no reason not to go along with them, and that is how the matter was resolved.

*

My first day back from Japan, I appeared with Dean Rusk before the commission charged with recommending to the

Congress a memorial for Woodrow Wilson. We proposed a center for visiting scholars, foreign and American, to be established in Washington. Maybe, from bits and pieces, the equivalent of a major university can gradually be put together in this city.

✳

The negotiations for the new cultural agreement with the Soviets are almost completed. There have been some minor revisions, designed to help prevent abrupt cancellations by the Soviets of tours by American groups. In the end, of course, there can be no absolute guarantee. No doubt, if they cancel another American tour in the way that they canceled *Hello, Dolly!* we could threaten them with war. Other than that, however, we can only cancel one of their tours or suspend the whole exchange agreement. One or another of these courses might at some time be necessary, I suppose, but neither, obviously, is a way to advance a policy of détente.

So there are limits to how tight we can make the cultural agreement. Important though it is, it is bound to be somewhat less enforceable than, say, the agreement to ban nuclear tests in the atmosphere. Curiously, however, this has not been an easy point to get across at the White House. The cancellation of *Hello, Dolly!* seems to have left an open wound. I'm told that the President took it as a personal affront, since "Hello, Lyndon!" was the theme song of his campaign. I don't know whether this story is true or not, but it's clear that a musical comedy is playing a surprisingly large part in an important international negotiation.

✳

John Gardner, Frank Keppel, Harold Howe and Philip Lee in HEW have been developing their plans for the Center for Educational Cooperation, proposed in the President's message, and we have been consulting at every stage. We have worked

out an excellent cooperative arrangement, and are now formu-
lating the drafts of two Executive Orders, one for HEW and
one for the interagency coordinating council, which I chair.
Frank Keppel particularly has urged us to put strong language
in our Executive Order, so as to leave no questions about the
authority of this coordinating mechanism.

❊

The cancellation of *Hello, Dolly!* continues to bother important people. I had a long call from the White House today.
They wanted a great deal of information about the day-to-day
workings of the U.S.-Soviet agreement.

❊

Secretary Rusk, Assistant Secretary Leddy and I, at long
last, went to the Soviet Embassy for the signing of the cultural
agreement. When I arrived, I learned that there wasn't going
to be a signing after all. A call from the White House had come,
at the very last moment, instructing us not to sign.

We went into lunch anyway, trying to treat it all as a small
matter. "Bureaucracy," somebody said, hoping that the Soviet
officials would understand that particular excuse. I was seated
next to Romanovski, my opposite number in the Soviet government, who had come to Washington for the signing. If he leaves
without signing an agreement, the incident will escalate in
importance, so I thought I had better try to persuade him to
extend his stay in Washington. I suggested to him that the
unexpected change in schedule might have its good side; he
could have a breather away from his job. Did he like to walk?
Washington was a good town for walking.

He came back with a question. "Do you walk?" he asked.

"Yes," I said. "I walk to the office in the morning. It takes
about an hour."

"I walk every morning too," he said. "About an hour. Do
you walk home?"

"No."

"I walk home," he said.

"In Washington, when I go home at night," I said, "it's all uphill."

"Not in Moscow," he said.

I think he'll stay a day or so longer, but not beyond that.

On getting back to my office, I discovered that the White House still had the cancellation of *Hello, Dolly!* on its mind. Under the projected agreement there was no ironclad guarantee that such an event couldn't happen again.

✻

Left for Peru, to attend a meeting of our Cultural Affairs Officers in Latin America.

Romanovski also left today. The agreement still isn't signed.

✻

Disagreement over the Education Officer proposal has become hotter. All the arguments from the Task Force days have been renewed. We had a heated meeting at the White House today about it with representatives of the USIA. They were worried, as they have always been, that the Education Officer would intrude on the prerogatives of their Public Affairs and Cultural Affairs Officers. I think we finally agreed on a job description, and also saved the fundamental principle, but the going was heavy. Each agreement that we make seems to come unbuttoned.

✻

I testified before John Brademas's Task Force today on the International Education Act. It's hard to believe his group belongs to the same legislative body as John Rooney's committee. Brademas's colleagues' greatest worry seemed to be that we weren't asking for anything like the amount of money that was needed. Were we serious or were we making only a token move in the right direction? There didn't seem to be any important difference of opinion between Republicans and Democrats on this point. Of course, in the end Brademas's group can only recommend that Congress authorize the spending of money for the purposes of the bill. Another committee approves the actual budget.

April, 1966:

Another long go-round with Senator Morse, who has studied our answers to his questions, and now seems ready to go to work in the Senate on the International Education Act.

❋

The Bureau of the Budget sent back the proposed Executive Orders for State and HEW on which we've been working. They don't know why we need new coordinating machinery—this despite the fact that both the House committee and Senator Morse have specifically asked for assurances that there would be close coordination. We now have to reargue the whole matter with the Budget people.

❋

The Congress is increasingly restive about the President's budget. The costs of Vietnam, it turns out, have again been underestimated. Our own difficulties in CU are aggravated by the fact that John Rooney is ill, and his committee hasn't been meeting. There's no telling when it will issue its report, permitting us to go before the Senate.

❋

The Bureau of the Budget has now finally indicated to us that HEW will not be permitted to fund the Education Officer program. Dean Rusk and John Gardner have both agreed that HEW should do so, but all of us have been overruled.

Obviously, Rusk or Gardner could go to the President on

this matter and perhaps make their point. But it isn't the kind of matter one goes to the President about. It isn't even the kind of matter on which one can get the full attention of Charles Schultze, the Director of the Budget.

The Budget people fear that if HEW provides the funds for Education Officers, there will then be a flood of requests from other parts of the government, each wishing to assign a representative to our embassies. The Bureau of the Budget has taken the line, therefore, that the Education Officers should be funded by the State Department.

This hurts us three times over. We don't know when we'll be able to ask for the money, since John Rooney is still ill, and so we can't go ahead with our recruiting program. And when we do have our chance to ask for the funds, we shall have to make the request to a subcommittee that has given no sign that it is aware of the existence of the President's program in international education. Congressman Fogarty's committee, which would have handled a request from HEW, would be in a much better position to appraise the request, since it would also be examining the budget for the International Education Act if that Act is passed. I must now rest my main hope on a personal appeal from the President to Rooney, and I've asked the President's assistants to ask him to make it.

✳

The mood on Capitol Hill gets worse. I was told that some Senators, looking over one of the Administration's proposals in a closed committee meeting, agreed that the motto of this Administration should be: "We shall overdo."

✳

In redoing the drafts for the Executive Orders to insure coordination of the international education program between HEW and State the work has been passed down to people at lower levels. As I feared, jurisdictional worries have reappeared.

The problem is further complicated by the fact that there have been changes of personnel over in HEW, and the new people have to be brought abreast not only of the facts, but of the spirit of the operation. I had a meeting in my office today with some of these new people. I think that I may have succeeded in allaying their suspicions, but I'm going to have to keep at it.

May, 1966:

At the reception for the Diplomatic Corps at the White House, Senator Fulbright was a couple of places ahead of me in the line going past the President. The President, smiling broadly, pulled a piece of paper from his pocket and read it aloud to the Senator. It was a note from the President's cook, telling him that he was to keep to his diet and eat what he was given without complaining. "Can a man who gets notes like this from his cook," the President asked Fulbright, "be suffering from the arrogance of power?"

The President was good-humored about it, and Fulbright laughed. But the President missed the point of Fulbright's lectures on "the arrogance of power" if he thought that the issue they raised was a personal one.

❊

The Brademas group has reported favorably on the International Education Act.

❊

The cultural agreement with the Soviets was finally signed— in Moscow. The document was exactly the one that was ready to be signed in Washington six weeks ago.

❊

I addressed the Executive Board of UNESCO in Paris today. My subject was the new international education program, and

I stressed the fact that the President had singled out UNESCO as an international organization with which we intended to cooperate. The Director General, René Maheu, read portions of the President's Smithsonian Address aloud and reminded the Board that he had called their attention to the speech at the time it was delivered. "These are the ideals of UNESCO," he said. I believe the Board is impressed and hopeful.

＊

Arrived in Belgrade and have had a number of successful sessions with the Foreign Minister and the Minister of Education. We are going to establish binational planning teams, made up of professors appointed by scholarly societies, to review the entire range of Yugoslav-American educational relations.

These planning teams, which I set up to review relations in a number of countries, look as though they are going to produce even better results than I had hoped. It is particularly gratifying to know that we will have such an arrangement with Yugoslavia. The chance to set an example of close, businesslike cooperation with a socialist country is very important. I only wish that we had a little more money to support the program.

June, 1966:

The International Education Act has passed the House. I'm delighted, of course, but not quite so delighted as I thought I'd be. It isn't only that the outlook for this Act in the Senate is still uncertain. It's the general atmosphere. My job, though I enjoy almost every minute of it, is like a small pinpoint of light in the surrounding gloom. The war is on my mind almost every minute I'm not at my desk. It's on everybody's mind, and nervousness about the cities and the prospects for the federal budget aggravate the situation. This has become a sullen, mean-tempered city. And yet only last year at this time this Administration was riding high.

❊

Still no report on the CU budget. John Rooney is very ill. Beginning July 1, our funds will be provided by a continuing resolution of the Congress. This holds us to last year's figures, but means that, in spending the money, we have to guess what Congress will eventually do. If we spend at last year's rate and they cut us, we'll be in trouble.

July, 1966:

David Bell, the head of AID, is leaving the government after more than five years' service. We had a farewell party for him today, and I thought that he was already looking better. George Ball will be leaving soon too. Frank Keppel has already left.

❊

The riots in Cleveland are fearful. I said to one of the people in the White House that I thought that Vietnam had something to do with the mood in the cities. He is a sympathetic and sensitive man, but he looked surprised that I should think anything of the kind.

❊

I saw Dean Rusk today to discuss a number of matters. The minor issues took only a few moments. Then I turned to the question of Education Officers and Cultural Affairs Officers, suggesting that since the Education Officer proposal was hitting roadblocks, we should review the relationship of the Cultural Affairs Officers to the Information Agency, and try to free them from their subordination to propaganda. But while I talked, cables were brought in to him twice, and we were interrupted by a telephone call from the UN mission in New York. Once again, it wasn't the moment to try to pin him down to a campaign of action about cultural affairs. The decision was left hanging in the air.

I had hoped, too, that I would have a chance to talk to him about Vietnam, even though it's not in my official domain. But then there was another telephone call from a harried ambassador in Europe, following which, to my surprise, the Secretary leaned back, stretched wearily and turned to me. Rushed as we always were, he said, we never had a chance to say the things that wanted to be said, and he hoped I knew that he thought I was doing a grand job. I was touched by his words and said so. Then the phone rang again, I looked at my watch and at the pile of papers on his desk, and took myself out of his office.

August, 1966:

Senator Morse has indicated that he is thinking of submitting his own bill in lieu of the International Education Act. I think we have convinced him that there are no ulterior purposes in the Act, but nevertheless he would like new language to provide still stronger guarantees against federal penetration of educational institutions. I would prefer an amendment to the Act, if he thinks it is needed, rather than an entirely new bill, which would have to go back to the House, and might not go through. Besides, time is growing short.

But Morse's instinct is sound. He thinks that perhaps an independent body, composed of academic organizations, could be created, which would directly administer funds for international education programs in place of HEW. I don't see great dangers in the International Education Act in its present form, but his idea is even better. However, last fall when I raised the idea of establishing such a semiautonomous body in discussions within the executive branch, I found few takers. I doubt that either the Administration or Congress is ready for it. The International Education Act is a good substitute.

※

Senator Morse is moving ahead with the International Education Act in substantially its present form, and hearings began today. They went well. John Gardner was the first witness, and I followed him. Senators Morse and Yarborough were particularly cordial, and Senator Javits's questions were astute and helpful. Senator Morse hopes to get the bill to the floor right after Labor Day.

※

The Senate hearings on the International Education Act have been suspended. Other matters have the Senate's attention. The old hands around here tell me that they can't remember when the mood in Washington was so irritable. Even if the Administration were free to focus its efforts on the cities, I don't know how much support it could get from the Congress.

September, 1966:

I sat with John Gardner tonight at a public dinner, and he told me that the outlook for the International Education Act isn't good. Congress is rushing to close up shop, and it may never get to the bill, which doesn't have high priority. I told him I would get to work on the problem immediately. The White House has told us that if we're going to get the Act passed in this session, we'll have to do it on our own. The President has other problems on his tray.

※

This evening in New York, Senator Fulbright gave the principal speech at the closing banquet of the symposium called to celebrate the twentieth birthday of the Fulbright program. He talked almost exclusively about "this savage war" in Vietnam. When he finally turned to educational and cultural affairs, he said some graceful things, but concluded with the pessimistic prophecy that, as long as the war went on, he saw a dim future for international education and cultural exchange. It was hardly a message of celebration, and it saddened everybody. And of course he is very possibly right. But we're still in the middle of the struggle for the new international education program, and we can't back away from it. As the speech illustrates, the problem is to catch even a corner of people's attention.

❋

Paul Miller has taken over Frank Keppel's job as Assistant Secretary for Education at HEW. He and I breakfasted with Senator Morse this morning. The Senator was all business. He thinks he can get his committee's calendar cleared, and will try to get the Act to the floor in time for the Senate to act on it. He will have a final day of hearings in a week or so.

❋

I addressed a meeting of the trustees of the Social Science Research Council. One of them, an old colleague of mine from Columbia, congratulated me for what I was trying to do, said that he approved of my policies completely, and predicted that I would be out of the government in six months if I insisted on sticking to them.

❋

Had breakfast with Senator Fulbright. He listened sympathetically to my discussion of the International Education Act, and said that the problem with the Act was that people hesitated to give this Administration any more broad powers. But he said that he would support it. He asked me about other aspects of my job, and he laughed when I said something about "this lunatic city."

"Well, well," he said. "It may have been worthwhile, after all, to bring you here. It's expensive, I admit, but we have to do something to give professors an education."

*

Mr. Rooney is back, after a lung operation.

*

Senator Morse concluded hearings on the International Education Act today.

*

The Rooney committee issued its report today. Our request has been cut 5 percent, and since the Bureau of the Budget had cut us 5 percent below last year, the total reduction is about 10 percent. My hunch is that the Rooney committee had long since made up its mind to cut our budget by about 5 percent no matter at what figure we came in. So, with the help of the Bureau of the Budget, we may have given away 5 percent.

October, 1966:

I testified on CU's budget before the Senate Appropriations Committee today and asked that the funds cut by the House be restored. I'm not optimistic. The Secretary had appeared before me, and the discussion had got into our touchy relations with France. When I took the chair, I was immediately challenged to show what benefits accrued to the United States from the cultural program with France. Once more, I controlled my instincts. I didn't say, though I wanted to, that General De Gaulle had never been an exchange student.

*

I left today for Jordan, Israel and Tunis. Then on to Paris and the UNESCO general conference. It looks as though there's finally agreement on the delegation, of which I'm to be chairman, but the appointments aren't yet official.

❄

A call came through to me today from Washington telling me that our recommendations for the UNESCO delegation have been rejected, and that a new delegation is being formed. The reason, I am told, is that the President didn't like receiving recommendations at the last moment. This stunned me, not least because my office started these recommendations through the mill many months ago and has been pushing to get them accepted. But we seem to be licked. I confined myself, in my calls to Washington, to arguing only that certain individuals who had been on the list were indispensable. In one case, a man has been cut from the list whose presence is required by law. I think I made at least that point successfully.

❄

Our visit to Tunis has been particularly fascinating. Chadli Klibi, the Tunisian Minister of Culture, remarked to me: "We are a poor country. For us especially it is important to have an ambitious program in the arts."

There is much that we could do in concert with the Tunisians, in both the arts and sciences, particularly because we have large reserves of surplus currency here. The problem is to get Congress to authorize us to use them.

❄

I have stopped in Rome to attend the meeting of the executive directors and representatives of the governing boards of the binational Fulbright foundations in Europe. I continue to be impressed by the quality of the people from other countries who have become involved in the administration of the cultural programs with the United States. It is obvious that, despite their criticisms on matters of detail, many of which are justified, they are basically satisfied that these programs are not one-sided

American efforts to brainwash them, but are genuinely cooperative and binational. France, the U.K. and Germany all make
substantial financial contributions, and the smaller countries
are also beginning to do so. Yet they also have their own programs in addition, to which we make no contribution.

What is causing a grave problem, however, is that we in
Washington have generated a feeling of insecurity in Europe
about the permanence of our intentions with regard to the exchange program. In part, this is the consequence of the actions
of the Appropriations Committees in the House and Senate,
which deal with the program in a way that is bound to seem
arbitrary in Europe. And, in part, it is the consequence of the
general feeling in Europe that the United States has become
preoccupied with other parts of the world.

❋

The Senate Appropriations Committee, I learned in the
course of a telephone conference with my office in Washington,
made an effort to restore half of the reduction imposed by the
House, although the restoration was entirely in foreign currencies. However, in conference with the House committee,
the House remained firm and this provision was struck down.
So the original cut—over 10 percent—prevails. Since we have
also used up reserve funds we had accumulated, the effective
budget for next year for CU has been reduced by close to 15
percent. So far as I am aware, the fact that the President has
announced to the world a new American program for international educational cooperation has not even been mentioned
in the entire Congressional debate over the CU program. "Only
connect," E. M. Forster says somewhere. But the government in
its deliberations doesn't connect things that are related, and it
connects things that aren't. Thus AID is under suspicion now
because people are angry about Vietnam. And CU is commonly
criticized as another kind of AID program, though it isn't
basically that kind of program at all.

But perhaps the International Education Act will fare better. It goes before other groups in Congress, and I've learned not to think of either house as a single body.

❋

I have arrived in Paris for the UNESCO general conference and have met the people on the delegation. With a couple of exceptions, it's an entirely different delegation from the one that I thought had been named when I left Washington. I am very disturbed that the people on the original slate, gifted and devoted people who had already made their preparations to come to Europe, were treated so cavalierly. Now we have a delegation not all of whom have arrived, and many of whom will be able to spend only a few days here. I don't understand making appointments of this sort; it makes no political sense, and it hurts us seriously at an important international meeting. Whatever the reason—whether it was anger at bureaucratic delay, dislike of some of the people on the original list or a desire for new faces—the whole affair smells of capriciousness and pique.

And yet, in fairness, it has to be said that the new people look very good indeed. The White House keeps surprising me—first, by the way in which it turns down people of high quality, and then by the way it comes up with people of high quality.

❋

The International Education Act passed the Senate today. There's only one week to go, however, before the adjournment of Congress. The Appropriations Committees will have to act very fast.

❋

The Congress adjourned today. The Appropriations Committees took no action on the International Education Act, so that we have the legislation but no funds for it. The effort to get the funds and to make the Act real will now have to wait for the new Congress in January.

I find that I am asking myself once again whether there is any point in staying on in the government. The prospects for what I have been trying to do look steadily dimmer, and the war, despite the official calls for peace and rumors of negotiations, grows steadily more hideous. But I don't like to back out after having given the effort so short a trial. I've made up my mind, and have told Helen, that my staying in the government will depend on whether I can get the White House and the President himself to put on steam in relation to international education—for example, by pressing the case personally for the CU budget and the Education Officers with John Rooney. How much does the President really care about the program he's recommended?

In any case, unless Vietnam policy changes radically, I won't stay past the end of 1967 at the latest. Nineteen sixty-eight will be a campaign year, and I can't see myself penned up in the government, unable to say in public what I think.

But as of now, dim though the prospect looks, I've still got a fighting chance to help accomplish some important and lasting things. They certainly won't be accomplished if I leave, and I don't want to have to say to myself that an opportunity was lost for lack of trying.

November, 1966:

The Congressional elections took place yesterday. The Democrats lost forty-seven seats in the House. Most of the people defeated for re-election were Democratic liberals. The Administration has lost not only support, but some of its most enlightened support.

10

Reasons of State

Karl Marx held the view that the material conditions of men's daily work have more to do with shaping their outlook than the philosophies they learn at school. If people inside government and people outside it don't see eye to eye, it may have to do with differences in the material conditions of work.

The outsider, and particularly the intellectual observer, usually has a large measure of control over his working schedule, and he has nobody to boss, cajole or tame besides himself. Moreover, when he looks at foreign affairs, it is ordinarily a leisure-time activity, unless, of course, he is a foreign-affairs specialist. So there is a certain amplitude in his view of the world. He can think of it as pliable and amenable to the application of thought, and he can feel that with good will and intelligence all sorts of things can be arranged or rearranged. He lives at the opposite pole psychologically from the man for whom it is enough just to get through the working day in one piece.

But that is the life, in large part, of the State Department official. From where he sits—from where he runs—the world is less tractable, insanity and cruelty are at its very heart, and a day is a series of crises. And the immediate imperative, the game that he plays every day, is to get through each crisis in good enough condition to be able to face the next. Not all the behavior of the people who work in government can be explained by the immense drifting inertia of the system in which they work, its methods of keeping them informed, or the curious culture of Washington. Some of their behavior is explicable simply by the nature of the problems with which they deal— in a word, by what are commonly called "reasons of state."

"If you can't stand the heat, get out of the kitchen," said Harry Truman. The most obvious necessity that weighs on a government, of course, is the necessity to say "No." With the best intentions in the world, a government of course has to be deaf at times. It cannot be responsive to all the demands upon it, for many of them are mutually incompatible. But the necessity to choose, which is also the necessity to reject, is only the basic necessity that hangs over people in government.

It is other necessities that give government service its recurrent quality of irony. For example, it is right to do the right thing, but it can be wrong to do too many right things at once.

Should scholars, scientists and artists from Communist countries be encouraged to attend scientific and cultural meetings in the United States? I thought so, and so did others in the Administration, including the Secretary of State, the Attorney General and the President. But the immigration law contained a provision that people associated with Communist organizations could not be admitted to the United States without receiving special waivers. This provision naturally affected almost all those who might come from Communist countries. And since it was a new law, which was far more liberal than its predecessor, and which had been passed after great difficulty, we thought it unwise to try to amend it.

To carry out our policy, we concentrated, therefore, on working out new administrative procedures for the issuance of waivers so that people from Communist countries could receive visas with a minimum of red tape. President Johnson's message on international education contained instructions to the executive branch to develop such procedures, and shortly thereafter we installed them. "The evidence of effectiveness" of the new system was gratifying. We received three or four favorable editorials and one or two kind words from friends. Most important, complaints dropped off sharply that distinguished physicists, poets or composers had encountered delays or indignities at our consulates abroad.

However, the system soon ran into a difficulty. A group of New Yorkers invited a prominent Cuban dancer to take part in an artistic festival, and while the lady's artistic attainments were unquestionable, so was her loyalty to the Castro government. Even so, few of us, looking at this problem all by itself, saw strong reasons not to admit her. The trouble, unfortunately, was that the problem could not be viewed as an isolated one. The State Department, at just that moment, was engaged in a major effort to win Congressional approval for the expansion of trade with Eastern Europe, and one unpleasant incident involving a foreign Communist admitted to the country in consequence of freer policies could upset this effort. We decided to take a chance just the same, but I still remember the weary voice of one of the government's highest officers as he said to me, "Very well. I don't give a damn about keeping this character out. I think we look foolish if we do. But if there's trouble, and the East-West agreement is lost, you're not going to sleep at night. Either your own conscience will keep you up or I will."

Repeatedly caught in this kind of situation, I found myself thinking about problems as I had not thought about them when I was on the outside. Timing, the measurement of how much you can get away with at any particular moment, is an unavoidable imperative of official life. This is why an official may seem deaf when, in fact, he isn't. The man on the outside who has an idea or complaint usually has only that one idea or complaint on his mind at the time. But the official has a number of balls in the air. He is engaged in a juggling act. For him, the problem is not the simple one of deciding between doing the right thing and doing the wrong thing. The problem is to decide which of the beautiful balls in the air he will try to catch and which he will allow to fall to the ground.

Moreover, the balls he is juggling aren't necessarily balls that he himself has put in the air. Deciding to enter the government is like deciding to marry a girl with a large, old-fashioned family: a man takes on an extensive set of commitments. The Secretary of State, a Cabinet officer across town, perhaps the President himself, have caught him up in the bargains they have made. They aren't necessarily explicit bargains. Often, they exist merely by implication. But they have some of the force of formal bargains just the same. If a group of conservative Senators have promised to give their support to the Administration's new housing program, a man at the State Department can't take them on, during the same month, in a battle over tariffs. If one Assistant Secretary's appeal to union leaders has been successful in inducing stevedores to drop their objections to unloading "Communist" tobacco from Yugoslavia, the Assistant Secretary for Cultural Affairs down the hall is ill-advised to try to persuade these same gentlemen immediately thereafter to withdraw their opposition to visits to the United States by Soviet labor leaders.

Only too often, this is the sad, unspoken story behind the apparent unresponsiveness of the government official to the ideas of the outside observer. The official is like a poor man drawing up a budget for his family. He doesn't disagree with the proposition that his children should drink a quart of milk a day; he hears the doctor's advice only too well. But he has a sick mother, and an unpaid debt to the loan shark on the corner, and his children also need shoes; so he cuts down their milk ration. "Politics," that disagreeable word, stands, in the first instance, simply for budgeting—for arranging that schedule of expenditures in energy, friends and influence that fit one's opportunities, resources and inherited obligations. In the process, something has to give.

Another trick which necessity plays on the official is to tie him up in principles—not his own principles, and not principles that are relevant to the problem he has to solve, but principles with which he has to live and make his peace just the same.

In my corner of the State Department, for example, I had an almost daily bout with the frustrating problem of surplus foreign currencies. These currencies should not have been a problem; they should have been an opportunity. They were a problem because Congress and the executive branch were at loggerheads over a matter of principle.

In a number of countries in the world—India and Tunisia are two examples—the United States government has accumulated to its credit, as a result of the sale of surplus commodities, large amounts of foreign currency which it cannot take out of the country but which are in excess of what it will require to meet its ordinary and normal needs. By allowing these "excess currencies" to go unused, we are, in all probability, allowing them to disappear, since in most of the countries concerned their value is steadily depreciating as a result of inflation. Yet an unsettled argument between Congress and the executive branch prevents the use of these funds. The Congress's right to vote appropriations is its ultimate weapon against the Executive. It is naturally disinclined to dilute this right, and, in consequence, it usually insists that the executive branch incorporate its request to use excess currencies into its regular budgetary proposal. But the executive branch, on the other hand, is usually unwilling to make its request to use foreign currencies in this manner. To do so, in its view, would be to give the executive budget a misleadingly swollen appearance; in particular, it would leave the false impression that tax revenues that could be used for a variety of purposes have been specifically set aside to be used in certain foreign countries.

This clash of principles has never been resolved. By now it has acquired the rigidity of a clash between two tribes with different taboos. It means that, week after week, opportunities to do useful things are lost even though the money is there to do them, and even though that money will probably never be used for any other purpose.

And so it was my lot, during my service in the government, to have to turn down scores of proposals—from other governments, from American universities, from medical teams and research organizations—to cooperate with the American government in useful educational, scientific or cultural activities. I had to do so without regard to the merit of these proposals, and even though not a single tax dollar was saved by doing so. In fact, the quarrel is probably doubly expensive: since some of the things that could be done with excess currencies have to be done in any case, dollars from current tax revenues have to be found to make them possible.

Moreover, principles can make difficulties even when they are immediately relevant to the problem at hand. Many principles have a tendency to turn equivocal when they are actually applied to specific cases. That small nations should enjoy the same right to shape their destinies that big nations enjoy is a principle, for example, that most people would accept. But it is easier to enunciate this principle than to stick to it—and small nations have as much trouble in this regard as big ones.

The Minister of Education of a new country called on me in my office one day and expressed his country's hope for educational assistance from the United States. "But before we go into details," he said, "I think I should make one point plain. We hope you can help us, but we do not want you to tell us what we should do. We want to develop our own plans and set our own goals. And then, if these appeal to you, we hope that you will see that it is in your interest to give us help."

I said that I thoroughly agreed with his way of putting the

matter. We would not wish to give educational assistance if it could be interpreted as an effort to impose our ideas. The question, therefore, was a simple one: What were his country's plans?

To this he replied: "That is the difficulty. We don't have enough trained people. We thought you could help us draw up the plans."

The standard problems in foreign affairs, and in government in general, present the decision-maker not with a choice between shining principles, but with a choice between the muddy alternatives available in a specific historical situation. Should the American government release all controls over movies sent to the Soviet Union under the exchange agreement? That is the direction, I think, in which our government should try to move: the government should not be a censor. Even if we look at the question from a propagandistic point of view, movies made in America that are critical of the American scene carry the message that we do not practice censorship. But the choice that I faced when, with others in the Department, I wrestled with this problem, was not a choice between censorship and its abolition. No matter what we in the United States might decide, the Soviet government exercised controls over what its citizens could see. Our choice, therefore, was to give Soviet censors sole control over the exchange of movies or to try to produce a fairer and freer exchange. If we chose the latter course we needed bargaining powers, and so we had to retain a residual right to share in the selection of movies under the exchange agreement.

What should the American government have done after the Arab-Israeli conflict in 1967? Should it have done nothing to help Jordan to rearm? Admittedly, traffic in arms is a dirty business. And arming an enemy of Israel, whose right to exist as a state has an American guarantee behind it, unquestionably seems dangerous and hypocritical. But that was not the way the problem was posed to policy-makers. King Hussein is a moderate

Arab leader. The policy-makers had to ask themselves whether they wished to allow conditions to develop that might bring his downfall, and how they could maintain relations with Jordan that might prevent the Arab Middle East from falling further under the influence of the United Arab Republic and the Soviet Union. If they made mistakes, these were mistakes in judgment, not inexcusable lapses from moral principles. Indeed, it is misleading even to excuse the decisions they made by calling them "necessary compromises with principle." They were efforts to translate a set of principles into practice within the limits imposed by a practical situation. A man who seriously wants to prevent bloodshed has an obligation to adopt a course of conduct which, so far as he can see in a dark world, has the best chance of achieving this purpose. And this means he must adopt a course of conduct which is actually available and not merely intellectually imaginable.

There is, indeed, an ultimate necessity that confronts a government. Does it wish to stop people from killing themselves by smoking? It cannot do so by prohibiting cigarettes. Does it wish to reduce racial segregation? It cannot do so by giving special subsidies to people who intermarry. In the end, a humane government has to make at least a limited peace with some of the folly in the world. It has to enter into a *mariage de raison* with unreason. It would be an enemy of any good purpose it might wish to serve if it didn't. The most difficult political problems are not political but anthropological. They aren't the products of a "system," unless it is the human nervous system and the human burden of history.

To be sure, when prejudices and myths obstruct the solution of problems that desperately need to be solved, a government cannot ignore them. But it can disengage itself only a little from the web of customs, sentiments, collective desires and conventional views of the world in which, along with those it rules, it too is caught. It cannot do so because it is composed of men who are the creatures of these ideas and sentiments; it cannot do so because, disengaged from the web of feeling and belief that ties it to its citizens, it has no way of ruling except through violence and terror. "An emperor," muses Hadrian in Marguerite Yourcenar's *Memoirs of Hadrian,* "can differ from his subjects only on a few points." He turns loose boundless fears when he tries to remake his subjects in accordance with his own rational master plan.

But what are known as "reasons of state" have their lighter side. I have not yet discussed the particular kind of necessity that gives life in government its induplicable tang. This is the unavoidability of the unnecessary, the certainty that the absurd, the bizarre, the trivial, will break into your routine every day, and exact a price if they are ignored.

"You'll be busy," said Miss Lovitz, my secretary, when I first came to work.

"I expect to be," I said. "I've got a lot of ideas I'd like to try."

"You'll be busy, anyway," she said. "Things happen. You'll see."

I found out what she meant.

In the midst of preparations for negotiation with the Russians on cultural exchanges, I was interrupted one day by news that an American mathematician in Moscow had found himself suddenly unable to control his indignation any longer, and had given an interview to the press denouncing United States policy in Vietnam. Attacking the United States from a forum in Moscow is not the advisable method for getting Washington's ear, but it is an excellent ploy if one wants to damage the exchange program with the Soviet Union. Our mathematician gave Congressmen who didn't like this program a chance to denounce it; and since, with mathematical impartiality, he had also gone on to denounce the Soviet Union as well, people in Moscow who were skeptical about the exchange program also had new ammunition with which to attack it.

It wasn't of ultimate importance. When the mild commotion

subsided, the exchange agreement had survived, and the professor no doubt felt better for having spoken his mind. The only damage was the wear and tear on a few officials like myself who had to repeat to irate Congressmen or irritated Soviet representatives that the gentleman was an American citizen with a right to free speech, including the right to say in Moscow what he could have said with as much practical effect, and with less damage to other purposes, in New York or California.

There is little an official can or should do about this sort of thing except shrug it off. Still, it takes time, energy and political capital to shrug it off, and the next time he appears before an Appropriations Committee some member of the committee is likely to remember that he didn't work up quite the degree of indignation about the case that a good public official should. The Soviet exchange agreement survives, the professor is unharmed, and the only damage is to the official's budget for exchanges with Western Europe or Latin America. This is the Carom Effect in government.

I am not given to animistic interpretations of my environment, but I began to think, after I had spent some time in the State Department, that perhaps there was something to be said for animism after all. It often seemed to me that an uncaptured Spirit of Mischief dwelt on the sixth and seventh floors. For it was absurdly unnecessary events that transpired which, more than international crises, produced the worn, resigned faces on my colleagues. We lived as though not Karl Marx but the Marx Brothers were poised outside our doors.

The history of Eduardo Frei's abortive trip to the United States in 1967 will illustrate the point. Dr. Frei, the President of Chile, is an exemplary representative of the democratic left in Latin America, and there were a dozen reasons why officials of the Alliance for Progress should have thought it useful that he make an official visit to Washington. But Dr. Frei's Parliament opposed his coming, and in the end he canceled the trip.

With that the story should have ended, but it didn't. A grace note of gratuitous difficulty was then added that bespoke the presence of a cosmic demiurge that won't leave bad enough alone. Suddenly, without advance notice, Senator Everett Dirksen spoke up and commented that the good Señor had probably only been coming to the United States to pass the tin cup. The delicacy of the remark was matched by its relation to the facts. Dr. Frei was the head of the only government in Latin America that had voluntarily discontinued American aid.

But what arrested my attention about this incident was not Senator Dirksen's error; it was my own feeling that he was in the grip of forces larger than himself. It hadn't been necessary for him to make a statement. He hadn't been caught unprepared by a reporter, nor was he in the midst of an angry Senate debate. No one would have noticed if he had said nothing. Apparently, the spirit just hit him. I couldn't help but feel, as I analyzed the event, that the spirit that hit him was not his own. He seemed as surprised and disturbed as everybody else when he looked around and noticed the nervous scurrying back and forth in Washington and Santiago that his remark had caused.

The most judicious people can be victimized. Joseph Palmer, Assistant Secretary of State for African Affairs, went to an African country once on a long-delayed effort to mend fences there. He turned up in the office of the President, and just after he had said how impressed he was by the country's progress, he was shown the transcript of Congressional testimony by Secretary McNamara, delivered the previous day on a quite independent issue, in which the Secretary had said, in passing, that the country was faced by a serious Communist threat. Yet Secretary McNamara was usually careful to avoid gratuitous utterances about the Communist danger; the statement seems to have crept into his testimony without his noticing. In fact, his testimony had never been cleared in advance, in accordance with the normal procedure, by the State Department. I recall

the stern face of Joseph Palmer's deputy at the Department
staff meeting, complaining about "bureaucratic inefficiency."
When I leaned over to the man next to me and whispered,
"Bureaucracy, hell. It's demons," my colleague brushed me off.
It isn't easy, in an age of science, to persuade people to look
at facts.

An entire conception of effective administration has been
built around the occurrence of the random and the absurd.
There are those who will tell you in Washington that there are
three levels of administration: "routine," which is handled at
the lowest level; "decision-making," which is handled by people
at the intermediate level; and trivialities, which are the business
of the man at the top. The Control of the Unnecessary may be
as good a definition of administration in a political environment
as any. The effectiveness of a government administrator is
not something that is easily measured from a distance, and so
a simple and available test is his capacity to stay out of trouble.
This is Washington's most usual test, and even administrators
who don't think it a very good test must manage to get a passing grade in it.

I did beat the demon once. A pleasant gentleman turned up
one day in the office of one of my deputies and told him that,
while he hated to make trouble, he had reached the end of
his patience. If something wasn't done to solve his problem,
he would tell the newspapers and everybody would be embarrassed. It seemed that he was the attorney for a chess player
who had been invited to participate in an international tournament in Cuba. The Department's passport office had refused
the player permission to go, but another office of the Department had given him permission to participate in the tournament
by telephone. He had done so, and had won second prize. And
now he wanted to collect his $3,000 for having taken part and
his $1,800 in prize money, but the government wouldn't let
him receive the money.

The attorney had tried a dozen offices, and one day the thought had struck him that chess, after all, was culture. So he had come to us. The player was a professional, the tournament had been taxing, and the government had said he could play. The equities, his lawyer argued, indicated that he had a right to the money.

My deputy told me about the attorney's visit later in the day. He tacked it onto the end of a report about other matters, and then merely by way of illustrating the inevitable inanities of life in government. He was surprised when I didn't let the story drop.

"Did you do anything about it?" I asked.

"Well, yes," he said. "I called a couple of offices at the Treasury Department. I found the character who's been saying No, and I told him it seemed unfair not to let the man be paid since the government actually gave him permission to take part."

"No dice?" I said.

"No dice. The character said that it was the State Department that had given permission. That wasn't his responsibility. His responsibility, in the Treasury, was to prevent business transactions with Cuba."

"Did you tell him that we're all part of one government?"

"No. I've been around longer than you have. We're not."

"Did you say it wasn't a lot of money—hardly a major business transaction?"

"Yes."

"Did you try anything else?"

"I wish that lawyer had never come in. I wish I hadn't told you anything about it. Yes, I called around in this Department, thinking maybe somebody had checked with Treasury, and perhaps it had been understood that the guy could collect his money. All I got for my trouble was an old maid in the passport office who said, 'People shouldn't play chess with Cubans.'"

I said that I was going to see what I could do about it.

"Now don't you get involved," my deputy said. "You've got other things to do."

I called a friend at the White House and told him the story.

"Stay away from it," my friend said. "It's not your problem."

I said to him that if the story broke, the government was going to get a lot more than $4,800 worth of bad publicity. And besides, I was tired of letting bits of unnecessary foolishness go by simply because I was too busy to pay attention to them. Just this once, couldn't we see if we could beat the system? Just a small, $4,800 beating?

A note of adventurousness came into my friend's voice. "I'll call the man in the Treasury Department," he said.

Fifteen minutes later he called me to say that he had reached the man, and the fellow had agreed to think about it. About an hour later, my friend called again. He was an old hand in government, the kind that is known as "unflappable." His voice had a hushed quality, as though he were whispering to a neighbor in church after listening to an unsettling sermon.

"The man did some thinking. I think we've got a deal, but I'm not sure. The Treasury will let our chess player collect the $1,800 because that's the prize money. But he can't have the $3,000 because that's payment for his participation, which makes it salary, which makes it *verboten.*"

We were both silent on the phone for a few moments. Then I said that, despite my lifelong admiration for fine distinctions, such a decision was going to make the government look more picayune than ever.

"I know," said my friend. "But the man in Treasury is worried about precedents. It's bigger than chess. He told me."

But I was persistent. I said that this case would be a precedent only if another chess player was refused permission to go to Cuba, and then was permitted to play, and then won second prize. That possibility wasn't going to keep me up at night. "Doesn't anybody have a sense of proportion?" I asked.

"Since you bring up a sense of proportion," my friend said,

"I think you should know that if this is going to be solved, it's going to take the intervention of the Secretary of the Treasury himself." He sighed. "But I suppose that's what we have Secretaries of the Treasury for."

It is. In a week or so I heard that the chess player had his money. But the Demon of Happenings came right back at me. That afternoon, Roger Stevens, head of the National Endowment for the Arts, called me about a conflict between the scheduled appearance in Mexico City of an opera company his organization was supporting and that of a symphony orchestra which CU was sponsoring. They oughtn't to appear in the same city on the same dates, Roger said, and I agreed. We were still in agreement when it appeared that they were scheduled not only for the same city on the same evening, but for the same theater.

Whether or not the Demon exists, there are certain kinds of people in the government, or around it, who seem to have a special ability to manufacture Happenings.

Some years ago, Isaiah Berlin took his cue for an essay on Tolstoy from a line among the fragments of the Greek poet Archilochus: "The fox knows many things, but the hedgehog knows one big thing." There are hedgehogs in Washington, people who ambulate slowly through the scene, encased inside the one thing they know. Today a hedgehog turns up in your office to tell you that rural electrification is the key to the economic progress of the poor countries; the next day another hedgehog comes in who believes that illiteracy, and nothing but illiteracy, is the source of the world's problems. At every White House citizens' conference, on most citizens' advisory committees and task forces, at more Congressional hearings than one would imagine, it is a good bet that some hedgehog will stand up and state his case: the recommendations of the committee on federal aid to education are useful, but there is nothing in them about aid to the left-handed; the panel on disarmament has done a thoughtful job, but its report entirely neglects the subject of moral disarmament.

One can never tell when some stolid country doctor from Iowa or some gleaming public-relations man from Los Angeles will turn out to be a hedgehog. And if he is, the Demon of Happenings is likely to be working through him. Say to a youth-is-all hedgehog on the staff of some Congressional committee that the government's cultural relations program has purposes that necessitate the involvement of some middle-aged people, and you will find yourself explaining to reporters, Congressmen and bureaucrats for the next month that it isn't true that you don't think people under thirty can be trusted.

In contrast with hedgehogs, foxes are more catholic in their concerns. They don't look on government as a place where issues are fought out or large purposes accomplished; they know that the real business of government is quite different. "If we look on men full-grown," said Thomas Hobbes, "and consider how brittle the frame of our human body is . . . and how easy a matter it is, even for the weakest man to kill the strongest, there is no reason why any man trusting to his own strength should conceive himself by nature above others; they are equals who can do equal things one against the other. . . ." That is the fox's view: politics is the struggle among men who are equal because they can do equal things one against the other. What counts is how to be among the hunters and not the hunted.

But the fox has a weakness. He has a tendency to insert himself into situations for the sheer pleasure of being foxy, and so he often causes trouble to no purpose, either of his own or of anyone else. On one occassion, a decent and understanding Congressman remarked to a colleague that he was worried that my office was going to change its plans and not send a symphony orchestra from his city abroad. Instantaneously responding to the sound of the hunt, his colleague called to tell me what would happen if I didn't do the right thing. "I'll get you up here before our committee," he said, "and find out what you're doing over there, and before I'm through with you, you'll be sorry you ever came to Washington."

The trouble was, my office had already decided to send the orchestra. The call forced me to think about it all over again, for it would have been disastrous to leave the impression that threats could make a difference. The original Congressman who had raised the question realized the damage the call might do. After his colleague reported the conversation to him, he rushed over to my office to try to set things right. His apologies were unnecessary, but so was the Happening that provoked them.

But there are other types who produce Happenings with more efficiency than either the hedgehog or the fox. One might be called the wild boar. He is the man, in the bureaucracy or in Congress, who simply stands fast, guarding his territory, his prerogatives, his prejudices. When these are attacked, he charges; and since he is easily inflamed, he sometimes charges even when people are merely passing close to his territory en route elsewhere. "Why did you send Earl Warren to Latin America?" asks a Congressman. One answers that the Chief Justice of the United States seemed a logical person to send to an international meeting of jurists. But the answer won't do: the man regards the whole Supreme Court as a conspiracy.

The most numerous of the superfluous types that inhabit government country, however, are those I came to identify as leeches. The leech has the same view of the world as the fox, but he reacts to it differently. He is moved not by the love of nipping but by the need for security. He fastens himself to the powerful in the hope of acquiring a little of their strength, and, just possibly, a job in the bargain. An official can tell when his star is in the ascendant in Washington. The leeches arrive. When his fortunes begin to decline, he sees them less often. There are officials who have welcomed their misfortunes for that reason alone.

Not that the leech is an ungrateful parasite. For the strength he receives, he tries to give some strength in return. He laughs when his patron laughs and worries before his patron is worried. And he offers a unique service: he reports what is going on in the darker crevices of the government. The leech's great function is to turn public issues into private intrigues. He can't tell you what the public problem is over which the President and a Senator are quarreling, but he can tell you that they are quarreling before you knew that they were, and he can tell you what the trouble *really* is. Needless to say, it is not what it seems to be on the surface: it is pique, jealousy, an old rivalry, a favor unreturned.

A leech whose friends had found a niche for him in the Department of State had a habit of asking to see me urgently, and then, when I couldn't hold him off, showing up in my office wearing a confidential look.

"You won't like this," he would say, "but I must tell you, because I am worried and I want to help you."

"What's the matter?" I would ask.

"Congressman Negative is very angry with you."

"I didn't know that. Have I done something awful?"

"You ought to have talked to me first. You spoke to Congressman Affirmative about sponsoring your bill. You should have talked to Congressman Negative."

"Well, perhaps I should have talked to you. But the fact is that going to Congressman Affirmative wasn't my idea alone. The President thought he was the man we should go to."

"You oughtn't to do such things without talking to me. I *know* these people. Now it will be harder. But I will talk to Congressman Negative. You know, there's a young lady from his state who wants a Fulbright grant. If I could tell him . . ."

"I'm afraid you can't."

"Then it will be difficult."

"Then perhaps you shouldn't talk to him."

The man would leave, puzzled and unhappy. And sometimes Congressman Negative turned out to be unhappy too. On the other hand, sometimes he had never heard about the whole thing and didn't care—not, at any rate, until the leech made him care. Then there were Happenings.

If government officials sometimes seem strangely abstracted, it is worth reflecting on their conditions of labor. It is hard to concentrate on the essence of issues in a world in which accident is the law.

11

A Second Chance:
Excerpts from a Log

November, 1966:

Back home from the UNESCO meetings. It's easier to consider the pros and cons of leaving this government when one
is a few thousand miles away. Here on one's own acres, it feels
a little like letting one's family down.

*

I went over to the White House for the talk I had resolved
to have with one of the President's assistants. I said that every
day I was growing one day older and sometimes more, and
that I couldn't hang on indefinitely merely hoping for results.
I thought the time had come for a push not only from me but
from the Administration in the areas for which I was responsible; I indicated half a dozen things that the President might
do, any one of which would be helpful, beginning with a personal talk with Congressman Rooney about the CU budget and
Education Officers. The President's man said he would try to
find the right moment to speak to the President.

I also reported that the war was increasingly a problem,

not only generally, but specifically in my area. It hung like a pall over us at UNESCO, even though we were successful in insisting on the principle that UNESCO was not a forum for discussion of political matters. Beyond that, the conversations I had had with Europeans, high and low, provided incontrovertible evidence, if we needed any more, that the war was doing the country's reputation untold damage. My friend listened seriously, I think. But Southeast Asia isn't his area.

*

I lunched with Senator Fulbright today and reported the doings at UNESCO to him. He said that it was a pity that problems of the sort we had been discussing couldn't be at the center of foreign policy. The war was like a bad disease; it infected everything.

December, 1966:

In Honolulu for a meeting of the Board of the East-West Center. I find that affairs in Washington are a little difficult to believe in out here. But I've been doing my best to explain them.

*

The long-range planning teams, composed of scholars who meet with scholars in other countries to work out five-year plans for intellectual and educational cooperation, are beginning to move into high gear. I met with the Yugoslav team today. I shall be meeting with the teams going to Brazil and Peru soon. Perhaps we shall make some progress after all in debureaucratizing cultural relations.

*

Congressional interest in the brain drain is developing. Senators Mondale and Edward Kennedy, independently, have raised questions about it with me. The former is thinking of a bill to restrict immigration from countries with critical short-ages in trained people; the latter is thinking only of holding hearings to explore the issues, which I think is less precipitate. In the House, Congressman Reuss is also looking into the prob-lem. I'm glad attention is being paid to the issue. It offers the opportunity to explore the whole area of cultural diplomacy and to analyze its purposes.

*

At the White House, I discussed the possibility of a bombing halt with one of the President's assistants. He told me all the reasons why and all the reasons why not.

*

Walking to work today, I slipped on the ice and broke my ankle. I wonder how Romanovski's doing.

January, 1967:

I'm getting around on crutches and making out all right. At a meeting of the Trustees of the Kennedy Center, people commiserated with me for having caught my foot in bureau-cracy.

Preparations are under way for the next summit meeting of the Organization of American States. I hope we can push edu-cation front and center. Sol Linowitz, the new Ambassador to OAS, is sympathetic.

*

Congressman Fogarty, chairman of the Subcommittee for HEW, died suddenly on the opening day of the new Congress. Without Fogarty the general position of HEW isn't what it was, and the prospects for funding the International Education Act don't look nearly so good. The blow is the more severe because

Fogarty's principal Democratic colleagues on the subcommittee, all of them supporters of HEW's educational efforts, were defeated in the election. The new people are much more conservative.

*

The President's address on the State of the Union was somber. Vietnam and the surtax were its main themes. We've come a long distance since last January.

*

I talked with the Secretary, preparatory to developing the Department's position on the brain drain. I'm happy that he is so strong on the point that the United States should not be a party to legislation or international agreements restricting the rights of individuals to travel and live where they please.

*

I'm told that the President will try to find the right time to talk to Rooney. No one's optimistic, but at least we'd be making the kind of effort we should.

*

The rumors of peace negotiations have turned sour. I've been privy to none of the details, but it certainly looks as though we've either fumbled an opportunity or been rigid.

*

Paul Miller and I met with Senator Mondale to discuss the brain drain. The Senator listened carefully as I told him about the study I had ordered, and the policy statement which the Inter-Agency Council on International Educational and Cultural Affairs was preparing. I tried to stress the fact that restrictive legislation was the wrong way out, and the easy way; the main thrust should be to promote educational development and an international circulation of skilled people. The weakness in my position, of course, is that we're not about to do anything like what needs to be done in this direction; so I'm merely talking about an abstract principle. The Senator wants to do something *now.* Whatever view he eventually takes of the problem, he's going to stay with it, of that I'm sure.

February, 1967:

The long-range planning team for Japan reports considerable progress.

I met with Senator Edward Kennedy and went over the main issues involved in the brain drain. He had no antecedent views on the subject, but he thinks that the attention of Congress and the public should be called to it.

*

I was called to a meeting this evening. *Ramparts*, it appears, is publishing an article revealing the CIA's covert support for international activities of the National Students Association, the Asia Foundation and other groups. I suggested that John Gardner should be brought into the review of the entire problem at once. The first reaction to this suggestion was surprise: Why Gardner? The issue had to do with foreign affairs and the intelligence community. I said that it also had to do with education, students and the independence of the intellectual community, and that the government's chief education officer belonged in the picture. The idea didn't float at first, but by the end of the meeting discussion had come back to it.

The whole affair is, of course, acutely distressing. After all the explanations have been offered—the atmosphere and needs of the cold war, to which the CIA program was a response, the freedom the recipients of the funds enjoyed precisely because they didn't know the source of the money, the enlightened and progressive enterprises that could be supported in this way—the questions remain. Why did the program continue for so long? Couldn't the dismantling of it, which began a few years back, have been pushed with more vigor and conviction? It isn't policy that explains this, but bureaucratic inertia and bureaucratic property rights. (The CIA isn't different from other bureaucracies, but it's better protected.) Still, couldn't the people in charge of the program recognize that it was bound to come out in the open? Was it necessity that compelled them to continue, or sheer bureaucratic insularity, reinforced by the monastic environment of covert operations?

And, of course, why did the support ever have to be given surreptitiously? Other countries have given such support openly. Part of the answer is that Congressional Appropriations Committees would probably have been unwilling to vote funds for the kind of activity CIA was supporting. CU, for example, has been giving open support to the National Students Association, and I have been criticized for it. But this answer only tells us how ossified the Congressional committee system is; it doesn't justify playing tricks, either on the public or on the Congress.

I didn't bring up many of these questions at the meeting, of course. The immediate problem was not to undo the past but to decide what to do next; I wanted to save my fire for the single suggestion, which I thought crucial, that the issue be faced as an educational one, and that John Gardner be involved. The reconsideration of policy, past and future, will follow if that's done. The idea of bringing Gardner into the picture might very well have come up in any case, but I'm glad that I could be present to be sure that it did. There are occasions like this—they usually come out of the blue—when one is glad to be around, and convinced that everything that one goes through is worth it just to have the chance to put in one's two cents at the right moment.

❋

Further meetings are being held on the CIA-*Ramparts* affair. A good part of the discussions have been concerned with the mechanical problem of communicating with our embassies abroad. The problem is to determine how to send out information most of which is still highly classified: Who should be on the distribution list? What information should be sent out? Should it continue to be treated as classified information? Yet the press in the United States and around the world has most of this information and is publishing it. Government is weird.

The President has appointed a committee to deal with the affair. Nicholas Katzenbach is chairman; the other members are Richard Helms, Director of the CIA, and John Gardner.

＊

In an odd way, the CIA affair may be the break in the weather that I've needed. It shows that our arrangements for dealing with educational and cultural affairs and with government–private sector relations are scattered, disorganized and misconceived, and it calls attention to the importance of the whole educational and cultural dimension of foreign policy. If the CIA was involved in cultural activities, I can hear people saying, they must obviously be important. The CIA program also shows that it is possible and desirable to support the activities of private nonprofit groups in foreign affairs while giving them maximum freedom and keeping the bureaucracy out of the act. Couldn't this be done in a fashion that was open and aboveboard?

It may be time to raise again the possibility of a semiautonomous foundation or commission to handle educational and cultural programs abroad. I have discussed the proposition with some of the President's assistants, and they show interest. The basic problem is that of combining accountability for the expenditure of public funds with the autonomy educational and cultural activities require. A sensible government, when it begins to touch the life of the mind, has to exercise the good judgment to erect safeguards against its probable bad judgment. It has to be willing to give people in these fields their head.

How odd it is—and how depressing—that the Congress has been willing to grant such autonomy when the government works through the CIA but has not been willing to give anything near such autonomy when the government operates through agencies working aboveboard. But the shock of this scandal may provide the opening we have needed to establish more sensible guidelines and more reasonable organizational arrangements for the support of educational and cultural activities.

The chances are surely two to one against anything new and productive being done in this melancholy year. But one chance in three isn't a bad chance in government. And if this foundation were created, it would represent the accomplishment of most of the original purposes I had when I entered. The disappointments we are encountering with the International Education Act and the proposal for Education Officers would seem much less important. I never imagined—not in my freest fantasies—that a chapter in the history of the CIA would provide an opening for a fundamental reform in cultural affairs.

＊

Paul Miller, who is handling the problem of getting appropriations voted for the International Education Act, tells me that he is running into roadblocks. Since Congress closed shop last fall without voting funds for the Act and since we are already halfway through the present fiscal year, he has asked for a special appropriation for this year to permit him to create the Advisory Committee called for by the Congress, and to develop the specific plans for a grant program for which Congress asked when it passed the law. But storm signals are up: the Appropriations Committees have been saying that this isn't the time to launch new programs. The money required is infinitesimal—some $70,000. That apparently doesn't change the story.

*

I rode down to Williamsburg with John Gardner to attend an international meeting, called to plan a conference on educational cooperation. James Perkins, President of Cornell, is handling the affair at the request of the President. The meeting is one of the remaining signs that the President's program is still around. On the way down, John and I discussed the CIA affair.

*

I've written a memorandum to Nicholas Katzenbach, saying that the CIA affair has two sides; first, to call a halt to what has been going on, and, second, to come up with a positive proposal for better arrangements. I outlined my view that a new foundation or commission be established to take over not only the programs CIA has supported, but other activities now scattered around in the government, including many of those in CU.

*

I am told that the budget outlook for CU is bad: the Rooney subcommittee is in a hunter's mood. We have asked for the same amount of money for which we asked last year, which is as much as we can ask in a year like this. Last fall, when we were fixing the budget figures, I had to ask the Secretary to intercede personally to support this approach because the budget officers in the Department didn't like it. He did so, agreeing with me that we shouldn't concede that the reduction imposed by the Appropriations Committees last year had left us at an acceptable level. But I doubt the Department's budget officers were ever really persuaded, even though they put through the request as I asked. At any rate, they are now predicting trouble.

I hadn't expected anything else. But I have asked the Secretary to speak to Congressman Rooney if he can, and have checked again about the President's intentions. I am told that he still hopes to talk to Rooney.

*

John Brademas and I met to talk about prospects for funding the International Education Act. The change in the composition of the committee formerly chaired by John Fogarty, together with the widespread feeling in Congress that new programs shouldn't be launched in a year when the Administration is talking about a tax increase, make him pessimistic. But he'll do what he can. What we're bucking, of course, is more than a feeling about the need for economy. It's weariness and a feeling of having been overcommitted, abroad and at home, by an Administration that enters ventures without looking down the road to where they may lead.

*

More meetings about the CIA affair. I have broached my ideas at a number of these meetings now, and people show a willingness to consider them that they wouldn't have shown some months ago. But we're still merely talking.

March, 1967:

Eugene Rostow and I testified on the brain drain before Senator Edward Kennedy's Subcommittee on Immigration. The hearings were quiet, almost scholarly.

*

The House Subcommittee on Appropriations held its hearings about our budget request today. I had thought (or hoped?) that they would bring up the question of the CIA and ask why the Administration had never openly requested funds for such purposes in the regular CU budget. By their raising the question,

I had supposed, they would have set the record straight as to whether the House subcommittee should bear some of the responsibility for the present shambles, which is what some commentators have been saying. But there were no questions about the matter at all, although it has been in the newspapers for weeks. The entire affair might as well have taken place on another planet.

Instead, the committee, and Chairman Rooney especially, went after me hard about grants that have been given to people opposed to the war in Vietnam. Not all their facts were straight —some of the people they were complaining about were actually supporters of Administration policy—but the basic question, of course, was a matter of principle, and I reaffirmed the right of grantees to freedom of expression. The case that raised the chairman's hackles most was that of a student at the East-West Center. Mr. Rooney had written me, saying that he would be watching this case with interest. I must say that he kept his word. The level of his voice never dropped below a shout.

The Education Officer request for next year was in the budget, but discussion of it was postponed. We are to have a hearing on our supplemental request for funds for the program for this fiscal year, and there's no point, it was decided, in going over the same ground twice. Of course, this delays our plans still further, even assuming, which I don't, that the committee will act favorably.

❊

I went back this morning to complete the hearings before the Rooney subcommittee. The subject was the East-West Center, and the case of the troublesome grantee was brought up again. But the atmosphere was calmer.

❊

Senator Ralph Yarborough asked to see me. He is concerned about the CIA affair, and is contemplating legislation—perhaps an amendment to the International Education Act—to provide new mechanisms for giving open support to private groups. I expressed my hope that the Administration would come up with a constructive proposal of its own.

❊

The cast finally came off my ankle. It took a long time to heal, I thought.

❊

The Katzenbach committee's report was made public today. It prohibits the CIA from supporting programs in educational, cultural and philanthropic fields, and recommends a new committee to develop a proposal for a more "mature" way of supporting useful international activities of private nonprofit organizations. It also spells out, albeit briefly, a couple of examples of how this might be done, and thus goes beyond vague platitudes. The President has accepted the report. This is all excellent news. I'd better stick around.

❊

The President has appointed a new committee to pick up where the Katzenbach committee left off. Secretary Rusk is its chairman, and Ramsey Clark and Charles Schultze, Director of the Budget, are also on it. Milton Eisenhower, Thomas Gates, Paul Porter and Herman Wells are some of its nongovernmental members. There is also representation from Congress —the chairmen of the Foreign Relations, Defense and Appropriations Committees in the two chambers, and the ranking minority member of Appropriations: Fulbright, Richard Russell, Carl Hayden, Milton Young, Thomas Morgan, Mendel Rivers, George Mahon, Frank Bow—an assorted group if ever there was one. The secretariat will be supplied by the Bureau of the Budget.

The Secretary called me in to ask me to work with him on

the new committee. We explored the basic alternatives that were open to the committee in preparation for my working up a memorandum on the issues. When the possibility of putting the Fulbright program under the authority of a new commission came up, he asked me what I thought Senator Fulbright's reaction to such a proposal was likely to be, and I said that I thought the Senator would consider it on its merits. Except for the committee secretariat, I shall be the only nonmember meeting with it.

The Secretary said that with all the other things he has to do he could stand not having this assignment.

12

In One Ear and out the Other

One evening, toward the end of my first year as Assistant Secretary, I concluded a long conversation with Secretary Rusk, and returned to my office. Repeatedly during the year it had been recommended to me from a number of quarters that I should reduce the amount of money spent on our academic exchange programs with Europe and use the savings for other purposes. I hadn't accepted these recommendations, but I wanted to settle the issue, and so had asked for an opportunity to go over it carefully with the Secretary. The meeting had been repeatedly postponed—more urgent problems kept getting in the way—but finally the Secretary and I had our talk. When I left his office, I believed the issue had been finally resolved, and that my view of the matter was now the settled government view.

I was, of course, wrong. Not fifteen minutes after I was back at my desk, a young lady, a junior official in the Bureau of the Budget, telephoned to say that she had been looking at the allocation of funds in my budget, and that she thought it would be a splendid idea to cut back the exchange program with Europe. That way funds could be found for one of the experimental projects in the new international education program that was particularly close to the President's heart.

I said that I would do what I could to find funds for this project, but that it would be a bad mistake to use the funds allocated to educational exchanges with Europe. "But why?" asked the young lady, and she proceeded to develop her case.

Since she was mainly interested in juggling lines in a budget and not in foreign policy, her argument had a somewhat abstract flavor. But I heard her out, and only when she was finished did I say, with what I think was good humor, that, by coincidence, the Secretary of State and I had had a full-dress discussion of the identical problem hardly twenty minutes earlier and had concluded that the exchange program with Europe should not be cut.

The young lady never paused in full flight. Treating the conversation I reported to her as the merest wisp of smoke in her path, she launched into a lengthy discourse: the foundations and universities had private programs in Europe, the Fulbright exchanges weren't necessary to maintain a favorable United States "image" in Europe, and, indeed, their precise function was unclear to her. She wound up by suggesting that it was time to do something "new" and to stop defending old-fashioned ideas.

The time was 7:30 P.M.; it had been a day of alarms, excursions and interruptions; I was due at an embassy dinner at 8:00 and had not yet changed my clothes; and the car had already gone for my wife. Perhaps I was a bit clipped. In any case, I incautiously asked, "Is it not enough that the two highest advisers to the President who are specifically concerned with this matter should agree on the way to deal with it?" The lady replied, her voice sharp with surprise that I should have asked the question, "No, of course it isn't. The Bureau of the Budget has to approve too."

On reflection, I wasn't surprised that she was surprised. After a year in government, I ought to have known better. The lady was merely trying to coordinate me, to make my thinking fit thinking at the center—which is to say, for that moment and that issue, her thinking.

And so we come to one of the great consuming problems of government—the problem of coordination.

The simple arithmetic of the American government's operations makes it hard to achieve consistency or order within it. In the course of a single day the important decisions made by the government are too large in number and varied in content to be made by any small group of men, or any ten small groups. So power spreads out. And as it spreads, more and more attention has to be given to keeping the different centers of power in touch with one another. Thus forward motion is blocked because time and energy have to be spent on lateral communication. The government becomes like an immense, somnolent animal that cannot twitch its toe unless it first moves twenty other parts of its body. And before it can do that, it has to undertake a laborious task of self-inspection. It must notice that its tail is tangled in its rear legs and unwind it; it must cure its right front foreleg of the tendency to move backward whenever the left foreleg moves forward; and, at the end, it must probably take one extra foot, whose existence it had forgotten, out of its mouth. By the time it has finished this process, the animal is often too tired to twitch its toe—if it can even remember that this was its original intention.

Indeed, the great Leviathan, government, has trouble moving until it has settled for itself, at least in a practical way, the classic philosophical problem of self-identity: Who am I? Which among this score or more of centers of initiative is the real me? Over the centuries philosophers and jurists have struggled with the so-called "problem of sovereignty," trying to establish where ultimate authority in a society lies and what the justification of such authority is. Those known as "realists" have usually said that it is government which is the sovereign, the monopolist of legal violence, the final source of order in the society at large.

These "realists" have been realistic only in the abstract. In the concrete, inside the maze of government, the problem is to find out where the power and authority are. It is to find them in all of their separate places and somehow make them work in one direction, within one coherent framework of policy.

It is a difficult thing to do. The problem of coordinating the government is one of the principal causes of governmental unresponsiveness. Why is the government deaf? It isn't as deaf as it often seems. Provided they are willing to go to the trouble and can find the proper representation (admittedly, two large provisos), most people can find a sympathetic ear somewhere in the government into which they can pour their woes. But in the government what goes in one ear has a tendency to go out another.

How can the government be made to act as one government and not as many? How can the phrase "the policy of the government" be turned from a wistful legal fiction into an actual fact? The search for a practical answer is responsible for some of the most conspicuous features of the Washington scene, beginning with the proliferation of a tribe of people I came to identify as the government's traffic cops. A particularly large collection of them, inevitably, work at the Bureau of the Budget.

The Bureau of the Budget may well be the most concrete contribution of contemporary American political science to the practice of American government. It was created in response to the need, long noted by political scientists and other observers, for an instrumentality of good housekeeping, lodged within the President's own executive office, which would permit him to control his Administration and prevent its separate departments and agencies from flying off, each in its own direction, like unguided missiles. The Bureau does considerably more than advise the President on the national budget. Its job is to make sure that each department or agency knows what its own special mission is, and that no part of the government duplicates the function of any other part. If it did its job with entire success, an American President could say of his Administration what God can say, according to the philosopher Leibniz, of the universe He has created: everything in it is unique and irreplaceable, nothing overlaps or interferes with anything else, and nothing good or necessary has been overlooked. It would be the best of all possible governments. At any rate, it would be the neatest.

Even though the Bureau of the Budget's actual achievement has been somewhat more modest, the idea behind its creation undoubtedly makes sense. I here solemnly record my conviction that the Bureau is in fact indispensable. Still, pragmatic political scientists should just possibly have given more thought to the way in which such a Bureau, in everyday, pragmatic reality, would have to perform its function. For the process of being coordinated by the Bureau of the Budget, when it is experienced from the inside, frequently has a bizarre quality. The President appoints Cabinet officers and bureau and agency heads to be agents of his purposes; his Bureau of the Budget, an extension of himself in his own office, then rides herd on all these people. The pragmatic consequence, in the everyday course of affairs, is that officials specifically chosen by a President to make decisions in areas in which they are presumably competent must explain and defend these decisions to people whom the President doesn't know, who do not negotiate with constituencies or foreign governments, who never have to explain themselves to Congress, and who cannot be called to public account for their political judgments. In a large government the process of delegating authority ends by delegating authority to God knows whom.

Of course, the President's appointed officials can appeal to him against the judgments of those who carry this delegated authority. But they have to be able to get to the President, the time has to be right, the issue has to be important enough, and they have to have some political capital in the bank when they do. Thus, in the interests of rational, well-organized government, Creon's secretaries (to use a phrase of Friedrich Dürrenmatt's) come to decide Antigone's fate. And while they can be stopped from sentencing her to public execution, it is much harder to stop them from nibbling her to death.

The tribe of traffic cops is scattered all over Washington —in the Government Accounting Office, on the staffs of Congressional committees, in the administrative section of the State Department. It is the need for coordination that explains their existence, their numbers and their earnestness. In fact, I had a number of traffic cops standing firmly at the crossroads in my own Bureau. One day, one of the ladies who kept the statistics complained to me that I had approved the idea of giving a grant to a young Indian professor which would allow him to enter an institute staffed by Americans in his own university in India. He had wished to prepare himself to teach American studies, and this device had seemed to me a cheap and efficient solution of the problem. But the lady, in a polite way, was wroth with me. She had categories on her statistical charts for Americans who went abroad, for foreigners who came to America, and even for foreigners who went to a third country. But there was no category for a grantee who stayed on his own campus. Could I not—should I not—reverse my decision?

A large collection of traffic cops also inhabit the seventh floor of the State Department, where they constitute the staff secretariat that sees to it that all the communications that reach the Secretary of State have been properly prepared, boiled down to their irreducible essence, cleared with all the people who should be consulted, and checked and re-checked to be sure that all the proper forms have been met. A memorandum came to me one day which I was asked to approve before it was transmitted to the Secretary. It was on a subject which seemed rather dimly related to anything I was doing, but it took less time to read the document than to explore the reasons it had come to me, so I dutifully read it and affixed my initials at the bottom of the page. A week or so later, the document came back to me. It had indeed been sent to me by mistake. Would I, therefore, erase my initials and initial the erasure?

But the severest test that I had to pass as a subject for co-ordination—the one that gave me the most trouble and I think the coordinators too—was in my relations, as perhaps I have already suggested, with the Bureau of the Budget. I don't think either I or the people in the Bureau were preternaturally stubborn. We weren't stubborn at all; we just had our own separate responsibilities, our own different ideas, and neither side would move. And I do have to confess that my ideas were bound to make life difficult for people whose function in the governmental process is to keep the traffic flowing smoothly.

For I believed, even though I was an official in the State Department, that international educational and cultural activities were good not only for American foreign relations but for the education of Americans at home. And plausible though this idea may seem, it doesn't quite fit the requirements for coordination. The Bureau of the Budget has both an international division and a domestic division. In arguing for my plans on the grounds that their potential benefits were both foreign and domestic, I was asking the people in the international division to make judgments that were not in their jurisdiction. I was inviting untidiness at the very center of good governmental housekeeping. Their usual reaction, inevitably, was like that of a schoolteacher directing a chorus who hears one of the children singing a different song. The teacher doesn't respond to the beauty of the song or the excellence of the delivery. The teacher responds to the fact of indiscipline and disorder.

Indiscipline and disorder—I had problems with them myself. I wasn't only one of the coordinated. I, too, was a coordinator.

And I noticed that I was one man when others tried to co-ordinate me and a rather different man when I was trying to coordinate others. On the evening I was sworn in, I dined with a friend who had held a high position in the executive branch and had established an unusual reputation for his impartiality and fairness. I said, merely in passing, that I hoped to avoid bureaucratic squabbles and had no intention of building an empire. My friend was greatly amused. "You'll be doing your job, won't you?" he asked. "You'll be trying to earn your pay, isn't that right? Then you'll be drawing lines, and defending yourself here, and pushing out there. That's what the job is all about." By the time he had finished his remarks I was happy that he thought I had just been kidding.

In fact, he probably didn't know how right he was. For as an Assistant Secretary of State I had very special obligations as a coordinator. The State Department has the responsibility of trying to bring some coherence and consistency into the myriad activities of the departments and agencies in the executive branch that have a bearing on our foreign relations—tax policies, immigration policies, monetary decisions, defense plans, scientific investments, copyright agreements, and a thousand and one other matters. And as a day-to-day matter, this task of coordination falls on the Assistant Secretaries of State. Each in his own area—Latin-American affairs, economic affairs, educational and cultural affairs—is the principal official responsible for traffic-copping the activities of other parts of the government that affect foreign relations. This responsibility is the largest single reason why the position of Assistant Secretary of State is commonly described, by those in the know, as "the dog's job" in the government.

For despite the Bureau of the Budget, despite the powers which Presidents have repeatedly assigned to the State Department, despite the repeated exhortations from Congress and from special commissions called together to diagnose the nation's ailments, the government remains a study in loose coordination. All over the government there are people just as principled—or, if you prefer, just as stubborn—as I was when at the receiving end of the coordinating process. And the government is organized in such a way as to provide them with excellent defenses, ranging from well-concealed bureaucratic foxholes to major legislative fortifications, that are designed to make their resistance to the process of coordination successful.

For years the Department of Agriculture has maintained a special staff of agricultural attachés abroad. Ostensibly under the direction of our ambassadors, they have nevertheless conducted a foreign agricultural policy only tenuously related to the foreign economic policies of the Department of State. The Defense Department has been an even more conspicuous semi-independent element in our foreign activities. It has functioned in this way even when the Secretaries of State and Defense, as in the Kennedy and Johnson Administrations, have been in firm accord that the State Department should be in charge of foreign policy.

These examples can be multiplied a thousand times, and they relate to small matters as well as large. In the course of making my study of cultural relations before I entered the government, I found tucked away, in a small corner of one of our major embassies, an office of the National Science Foundation, administering a grant program which probably equaled or exceeded, in terms of the number of people involved, the regular exchange program with that country. Yet the existence of this office was hardly known to the rest of the embassy, and the statistical information regarding exchanges ignored its activities.

Why is coordination so difficult? The answer to that question lies in the answer to another: What does a man in the government actually do when he tries to "coordinate"? Based on my own wrestling match with the problem, I came to the conclusion that "coordination" is, in fact, not one process but four rather distinct ones, each more difficult than the preceding.

At the simplest level, coordination consists in developing arrangements for the systematic exchange of information between different agencies, so that they can know what their partners in the government are doing and can adjust their activities appropriately. At a second level, coordination consists in defining certain common problems—for example, meeting requests from other countries for assistance in the teaching of English—and arranging to pool resources so that a concerted attack on these problems is possible. At still a third level, coordination means the adoption of common guidelines by different agencies, so that they act in accord with the same principles. If the Administration has decided to follow a liberal policy with regard to the issuance of visas, the Immigration and Naturalization Service in the Department of Justice, the Security and Consular Affairs section of the State Department, the Bureau of Educational and Cultural Affairs and all the geographic bureaus in the Department have to be brought together in a common interpretation of this policy.

And finally, coordination can mean adherence to a total, centrally developed plan, which has fixed the government's priorities, measured its resources and allocated responsibilities, powers and funds accordingly. This final level of coordination is the Platonist's dream of rationality in government. Unfortunately, however, coordination even at the simplest level—the exchange of information—is a hard nut to crack. In a vast and variegated government, the facts have a way of hiding themselves even when nobody is trying to hide them.

At one point in my service as a government coordinator, for example, I thought of creating a system for the exchange of information among the approximately thirty agencies whose programs might have an effect on the international movement of people in the sciences and medicine. I had friendly meetings on the subject with the representatives of these agencies and never had any question about the good will of all concerned.

But our meetings, nevertheless, turned out to have a curiously scholastic quality: they were more like meetings of casuists or lexicographers than of administrators or policy-makers. We kept having trouble about our definitions of "exchange," "migration," "skilled," "training."

Finally, I turned to the experts in coordination. I asked a man at the Bureau of the Budget to look into the matter and tell me what would be involved in setting up a useful system for the exchange of information among the agencies concerned. The man spent a few weeks looking into the question, and came back to say that it would take, as a rough guess, half a million dollars to conduct a study to find out if it was possible to conduct a study to find out what the government was doing.

Ever since that experience, I have had ambivalent feelings when I read news stories of Congressional investigations which have revealed such classic administrative blunders as the purchase of $24,000 worth of ordinary sea water for shipment to Vietnam. I am stunned by the waste of money, but I also wonder whether the investigation that disclosed it cost even more.

It is expensive, in the United States government, to find out what is going on. And it is not only expensive; it usually involves a laborious exercise in semantics. Some years ago, the Office of Education, in the effort to develop a basis for distributing federal funds, sought to determine the "average daily attendance" in the schools of the several states. More than ten years were required before the states could agree on a common definition of "average daily attendance."

Within the executive branch of the federal government, a similar situation exists. Before separate agencies can be brought together in an interagency reporting system, they have to agree on the questions to be asked and the vocabulary to be used in answering them. They have to decide on a common system of classification so that things that belong in the same category are put in the same category. And these matters of definition are anything but self-evident. The activities to be classified are multifarious, the purposes in terms of which each agency adopts a classification system are different, and the constituencies, the political requirements, the inner rationale of separate programs, are in conflict.

Indeed, the problem of definition is so difficult in government that semantics may take the place of genuine decision-making. In the fall and winter of 1965, when the Administration was planning the new program in international education, the war in Vietnam was already beginning to create budgetary stringencies. In addition, there were other problems. We recognized that if a new program was to start without delay, it could not be created out of whole cloth, and that existing agencies would have to be used. In response to these considerations, it was therefore decided that AID, which had a large budget and a going organization, should absorb a major part of the new program, reallocating a significant amount of its funds to international education. I question no one's good faith in reporting that the thought went through my mind a number of times during that period that we might be talking mainly about paper reforms rather than a genuine change in our overseas assistance programs.

For in my efforts to arrive at some reasonable way of measuring what could and should be done, I had already had an instructive experience. I had asked AID and other agencies to tell me what they were spending on international education, and I had been struck by the vagueness and variability of the criteria they used in answering. The answers had a now-you-see-it-now-you-don't quality. Everything depended on the meaning to be assigned to "international education." With the exception of the programs in CU itself, most international educational expenditures by government agencies were submerged in programs that had other names and purposes. Expenditure for a research program in tropical diseases might include a training program for laboratory technicians; a program in medical research in the United States might employ large numbers of foreign laboratory technicians. With the best will in the world, an agency answering my question could, within limits, stretch or compress its answers. Like Humpty Dumpty, it could make words mean what it wished; and to some extent it had to. Nor was there any easily available way for me to check the vast record and develop my own answers in terms of my own definitions. In consequence, we were proceeding within the Administration on a combination of fact, guesswork and semantic ingenuity when we drew up our estimates of current government-wide expenditures for international education. And it occurred to me that the same abracadabra could be used next year to show that new programs in international education had actually been introduced. I have little doubt, of course, that in fact real changes were brought about. But I also suspect that there may have been a few changes that were merely prestidigitators' tricks.

Daniel Patrick Moynihan, looking back on his days in the Kennedy and Johnson Administrations, has reported that when the new "coordinated" antipoverty program was being put together, the Bureau of the Budget, in developing its picture of what the government was spending, began calculating interstate highway funds as part of the financial aid going to cities. Was this flimflam, an attempt to make the government's program look better than it was? Mr. Moynihan thinks so: he uses the word "fraud." But another lesson emerges as well, and it applies just as much to honest men as to dishonest ones: the facts become elusive when the meaning of words is elastic. It just is the fact that the government often doesn't know what it is doing. For if it is to know—if, that is to say, people at its center are to know, and all the agencies that should also know are kept informed—a system of consistent and comprehensive questions has to be worked out. This means altering the vocabularies of separate agencies and developing a new filing and reporting system. It can be done, but the effort is often not worth the price.

Thus it is that when a man moves to the second level of coordination, at which he attempts to bring together a number of agencies to deal with common problems, he may well feel that he is walking on water. He cannot quite be sure just what all the agencies involved are really doing. And even when he surmounts this problem, he faces another: this is to arrive at some agreement about what constitutes "a common problem." For each agency is likely to define the problem from the point of view of its own special mission.

During my tenure of office, for example, I succeeded in bringing AID, USIA, the Peace Corps and other parts of the government together in agreement on a national policy on book and library programs overseas. This policy was formally enunciated by the President in a Presidential Memorandum, and thus acquired considerable official force. But it could actually be applied only within fairly narrow limits. The policy placed a *general* value on establishing libraries and encouraging the international flow of books. But AID has to think essentially of books that have a direct economic utility, and USIA is required, on the whole, to emphasize books that provide information about the United States. And so, if there was a request from a country in need of children's books, we were hamstrung. The agencies with the budget to buy books didn't have the adequate authority, despite a national policy, to fill such a request.

And at the third level of coordination, when the effort is made to bring separate agencies into accord with common policies and guidelines, all these problems become more severe. There aren't enough traffic cops to enforce the rules; more, the traffic cops often give conflicting orders.

Probably no better example exists than the efforts that have been made in the American government to establish a consistent policy with regard to international arms control and arms sales. The Foreign Assistance Act of 1966 states: "Programs for the sale or exchange of defense articles shall be administered so as to discourage arms sales." Yet the Department of Defense maintains an office of "International Logistic Negotiations" which has conducted a vigorous program for selling United States military equipment abroad, and which has been applauded by the Congress for the money it has brought to the Treasury. The head of this office was promoted in 1964 to the rank of Deputy Assistant Secretary as a reward for his success in promoting military sales.

Is this hypocrisy—doing one thing while paying lip service to another? The problem might be more manageable if it were. But the facts are more complex. They suggest that Congress and the executive, in one mood or another, in one forgetful moment or another, have established not one but several different policies. As a result of pressure from some quarters in Congress, for example, an office actually exists which is supposed to make the record of arms sales public. But thanks to others quarters in Congress, it has never received an adequate budget to do this job. Nor would such a report be easy to compile even if the money to do it were made available. Arms can be exported in numberless ways—for example, by licensing foreign firms to produce them. Thus not even customs statistics are sufficient to tell the whole story of the arms sales for which the United States, through its government or its private firms, is responsible.

But is there no central coordinating agency? Yes, there is. I quote from a report of the staff of the Senate Foreign Relations Committee, issued in 1967:

> Under the provisions of the post-World War II legislation concerned with the regulation of arms sales . . . the Department of State and the Treasury Department share the responsibility for establishing policy and for enforcing regulations with regard

to the sale of arms. As for the obvious connection between arms sales and arms control, the Director of the Arms Control and Disarmament Agency was given the responsibility . . . to "serve as the principal advisor to the Secretary of State and the President on arms control and disarmament matters. In carrying out his duties under this act the Director shall, under the direction of the Secretary of State, have primary responsibility within the government for arms control and disarmament matters."

But as the report goes on to indicate, the formal authority to coordinate is not the same as the real power to do so.

How and by whom the major decisions on arms sales are made is something of a mystery. There is reported to be a State-Defense Coordinating Committee for arms sales policy consisting of members of the Treasury, the State Department, the Defense Department, and presumably the Arms Control Agency and AID. Whether the full committee actually meets is uncertain. One thing is clear, however, from testimony the Foreign Relations Committee has already heard: the Arms Control and Disarmament Agency, despite its charter, does not sit at the high table when decisions on the sale of arms are made. Another open question is whether the Agency for International Development or the Bureau of the Budget actually participate in the process of making a decision to sell, for example, A-4B's to Argentina or have only the option of attempting to overturn a promise of arms sales already made to another country. . . .

Indeed, arms sales proceed not only with insufficient relation to arms control policy, but with insufficient relation to economic assistance programs.

Credits for military purchases are usually hard loans with high interest rates and a short repayment period. Development loans are normally just the opposite. Unless all credits to a particular country—both development and military sales—are subject to a comprehensive review, how can we know enough about the total economic circumstances of a country to make the right decisions? At the moment there seems to be very little coordination between the right hand of military export credit policy and the left hand of development loans.*

In sum, the problem of controlling arms races on the international scene may well be only a little more difficult than the problem of controlling arms sales within the American government. In the mild words of the Senate report, "The question that must be addressed is whether the governmental machinery designed for the management of our military sales program is adequate. . . . There is evidence that it is not."

Can a situation such as this be put down to bureaucratic inefficiency? Obviously, its cause goes much deeper. It reflects an imbalance of forces within the government and the country at large. "Coordination" is faulty because Congress or the President have failed to make the basic policy decisions they must make. And often they have made the conscious policy decision not to make such decisions. Faulty coordination, as often as not, is the product of the process of political concession. And it is useful to view the general process of coordination from this perspective. We can quite properly complain when, in an activity as important as arms sales, the left hand doesn't know what the right hand is doing. But it is the particular issue at stake that makes coordination a value. It is not, except for those who mistake neat organization charts for efficiency in administration, a value in itself. It has to be weighed against other values such as political harmony. And harmony is often achieved in a government by allowing its separate parts a certain looseness in their relation to the whole.

This is the ultimate reason why the dream of perfect coordination has to remain a dream. A master plan based on the rational assignment of priorities and the austere allocation of resources has its use: it reminds the policy-maker that concessions come at a price and that there are some concessions that carry too high a price. But neatness, consistency, economy,

* Committee on Foreign Relations, U.S. Senate, *Arms Sales and Foreign Policy.*

are not the only values in government. If a President contemplates liberal social programs, he may reduce the opposition's fears by leaving Mr. J. Edgar Hoover in place; if he wants a more liberal immigration law, he invites unnecessary trouble if at the same time he attacks Miss Frances Knight's position in the Passport Office. The result of such concessions, of course, is to introduce a policy which has, in fact, been only half-accepted. But that is where one calls on a "coordinator." The situation can be handed to him, with the instruction to turn the lions and tigers who have been brought together in this way into fellow players on the same team. He will do quite well, usually, if he keeps them from clawing one another to death.

Imperfect coordination, furthermore, often serves a purpose beyond that of maintaining political harmony. In some ways, it is more efficient than close coordination. Since at least the time of Franklin Roosevelt, the Administrations of successive American Presidents have launched new policies by creating new agencies, at the same time leaving old agencies in place. The new agencies bring drive and focus to the new policies; the old agencies persist underneath, like geological strata laid down in preceding ages.

Thus the American government possesses an Arms Control and Disarmament Agency although it also has a State Department, a National Security Council although it also has a Cabinet, an Office of Economic Opportunity although it also has Departments of Commerce, of Labor, and of Health, Education and Welfare. The result is an abrasive and cumbersome governmental apparatus in which enormous amounts of time and energy are spent in quarrels over bureaucratic property rights. Yet doing things in this way has at least two advantages. It reduces the resistance to new policies of groups whose survival would otherwise be threatened; and it gives the government the benefit of a new organization, cut loose from time-worn routines and doctrines, capable of attracting new people and able to approach its problems with a fresh sense of mission.

Admittedly, this opens the way to competition and buccaneering. But the chance may be worth taking when one measures the gain in energy and originality that comes from releasing men and organizations from the obligation to adhere closely to a master plan. Some of the most signal accomplishments of the American government have come from taking this risk. The National Institutes of Health, the Peace Corps, the National Science Foundation, are examples of agencies that have done well in considerable part because they have enjoyed generous grants of autonomy. American society is competitive and entrepreneurial; why should the American government be different?

A large part of the answer to the problem of coordination, in sum, is not to seek too perfect an answer to it. The value of coordination depends on the specific problem to be resolved and the specific purpose for which coordination is sought. If no agency by itself is strong enough to achieve an important purpose, coordination is necessary. It will consist in bringing separate agencies together to do what they cannot do separately. Similarly, if a bureaucratic tangle exists that frustrates the achievement of a stated policy—the subordination of Cultural Affairs Officers to Public Affairs Officers in the USIA hierarchy overseas is an example—then coordination is necessary. But in this case it consists in merely cutting the tangle, and giving those who are responsible for the execution of the policy in question a chance to do their jobs. Independence and pluralism are values; radical inconsistency is not. The essence of the problem of coordination lies not in managerial techniques but in the willingness of people at the center to make the necessary decisions.

What is more important than tight formal coordination, in short, is a clear and general understanding, throughout a government, of the spirit and direction of the government's policy. But it is here that we come upon a crucial problem. Confusion of policies is something the executive branch is pretty good at generating without outside help, but it receives an extraordinary amount of help from Congress.

Congress is not one body, or even two. Its committee system, together with the great power that Congressional rules give to committee chairmen, turns it into a collection of separate, semi-independent villages. And the seniority system that it uses to select committee chairmen makes it a form of government by village elders. Woodrow Wilson described this state of affairs more than eighty years ago. In its major features, it is unchanged.

The leaders of the House are the chairmen of the principal Standing Committees. Indeed, to be exactly accurate, the House has as many leaders as there are subjects of legislation; for there are as many Standing Committees as there are leading classes of legislation, and in the consideration of every topic of business the House is guided by a special leader in the person of the chairman of the Standing Committee, charged with the superintendence of measures of the particular class to which that topic belongs. It is this multiplicity of leaders, this many-headed leadership, which makes the organization of the House too complex to afford uninformed people and unskilled observers any easy clue to its methods of rule. For the chairmen of the Standing Committees do not constitute a cooperative body like a ministry. They do not consult and concur in the adoption of homogeneous and mutually helpful measures: there is no thought of acting in concert. Each Committee goes its own way at its own pace. It is impossible to discover any unity or method in the disconnected and therefore unsystematic, confused, and desultory action of the House, or any common purpose in the measures which its Committees from time to time recommend.*

What Wilson said of the House of Representatives applies, to a lesser extent, to the Senate as well. And so it is not enough

---

* Woodrow Wilson, *Congressional Government.* Houghton Mifflin, 1885.

that the Council of Economic Advisers, the Secretary of the Treasury and the Director of the Budget should agree that a tax increase is needed; nor is it enough that a majority of the members of Congress as individuals might also agree. One man, Wilbur Mills, the chairman of Ways and Means, must also agree. It is not enough that lawyers' associations, the federal judiciary and the Department of Justice are agreed that the courts of the country need to be expanded and that judges need more help. John Rooney, the chairman of the Appropriations Subcommittee that deals with the judiciary, also has to agree. Until he is persuaded, the courts remain overcrowded, and the work of the law is delayed and distorted.

As things now stand, one has to go around the circle four times—and they are four independent circles—before one has the approval of Congress. One goes before the House committee concerned with substantive legislation in foreign affairs or education or labor policy; one then goes to the parallel committee in the Senate; one returns, and makes one's case all over again, to the House Appropriations Committee; one goes back across the Capitol and tries one's luck with the Senate Appropriations Committee. And each of these committees has its pet projects and hates, its sense of jurisdiction, and its personal and political sympathies or antipathies toward members of the other committees concerned. It has been said that a camel is a horse designed in committee. What is likely to come out of this process can make a camel look like a greyhound.

So long as Congress remains many-headed, policy is likely to remain many-headed too. The purpose of coordination, properly conceived, is not to hold all the parts of a government in tight rein, but to clear the field of unnecessary obstacles and to give people who have a mandate to act the chance to exercise that mandate. Coordination is faulty not when people in government pursue policies and programs with a measure of administrative independence, but when men must go round and round in circles before they can succeed in getting fundamental policies defined or their authority clarified. Congress, which regularly complains about the lack of coordination in the executive branch, bears much of the responsibility for this condition. Few political changes could have as salutary and long-range an influence on the responsiveness of the American government as the reform of the rules by which Congress conducts its affairs.

13

The Sleepwalking Government: Excerpts from a Log

April, 1967:

We had our oft postponed hearing on Education Officers before the Rooney subcommittee today. It didn't take more than five minutes. "The nose in the camel's tent," said Mr. Rooney. "Another federal bureaucracy." "This isn't the time for a new program," said one of the Republican members.

So we departed. Scores of people have been involved in planning the program, hundreds of hours have been spent on it, and educators all over the country have been pushing for it—and it is disposed of in five minutes before a subcommittee that gave no evidence that it had studied any of the documents involved. Of course, the educators have been pushing at *me,* a man who was already convinced. They haven't done much concerted pushing on Congress.

But even if they had, it wouldn't be enough. They would still have to solve a mystery that has baffled everyone—how to get the Rooney subcommittee to examine programs rather than pick nits. Even though the Board of Foreign Scholarships, under the law, has general supervisory authority over the academic exchange program, we managed to arrange only this year for a member of the Board to testify before the subcommittee. The Board's representative appeared and read a statement. The subcommittee heard him in silence, asked no questions, and that was that.

I also had an appointment at the White House today, and told one of the President's assistants that I would be leaving before the end of the Administration. He was concerned, but took it gracefully. I'm to have a longer talk about it with others at the White House.

After we had finished our other business, the two of us took a brief walk outside the West Wing. He said that history would vindicate the Administration's decision about the war. It represented a fundamental new step in foreign policy and would make international stability possible. I said that we already knew what "history" would say. It was going to be written by men who were now among the young people demonstrating against the war. The President's man didn't reply to what I said, but went on to other matters.

An elementary problem in dealing with people at the White House is that so many of them seem so worn and frayed. Beyond a point, it seems cruel—and useless—to push them.

❋

Half the government was on the White House lawn this morning to greet the Vice President on his return from Europe. After the guns saluted him, he spoke and said that our friends in Europe were still our friends.

❋

I was told at the White House today that the President and Congressman Rooney have had a talk, as I had hoped they would. The Congressman angrily told the President about the opponents of the war to whom we were giving grants. The President appears to have been caught unprepared, and the conversation ended there.

I am meeting with the people in the Bureau of the Budget

who are acting as the secretariat for the committee, chaired by Secretary Rusk, which is to report to the President on new and better ways to support private organizations active overseas. Everything depends, at this stage, on the kind of document that is prepared for the members of the committee to study. If its focus is narrow, there will be, at best, a bale-and-wire proposal to create a new funding mechanism, and thereby save some of the organizations hitherto supported by CIA. If that happens, we shall have brought into being still another agency to be "coordinated," and one that will inevitably be known as the CIA orphan asylum. Worse still, its intention, I fear, will be to spread the gospel of American voluntary associations abroad. That, at any rate, is the gospel which some members of the secretariat are beginning to pronounce. I think it would be better to concentrate on educational and cultural exchanges in a nonpolitical context. Voluntary organizations belong in that context or in none, so far as government support for their international activities is concerned.

The question at the moment, therefore, is whether we shall prepare a narrowly conceived memorandum for the committee or a broader one, which pays attention to the disarray in our whole range of international educational and cultural programs. I have found the case for a broad review a difficult one to make successfully. The people in the Bureau of the Budget with whom I'm dealing, though intelligent, don't have knowledge-by-direct-acquaintance in foreign affairs and seem to me only dimly aware of the foreign sensitivities to which I am trying to call their attention.

*

In London, I have met briefly with Anthony Crosland, Secretary of State for Education and Science, and Wedgwood Benn, the Minister of Technology. The subjects were the brain drain and the technological gap—at bottom, problems in education and communication. Mr. Benn will be coming to Washington in a few months, and we shall see whether we can come up with practical proposals for working with the British that might be helpful. Donald Hornig, the President's Science Adviser, has taken a lively and enlightened interest in the matter.

❉

I had a talk with Robert Kennedy today. His concern about the cities and his bitterness about the government's failure to do what is needed have grown even more intense. I was struck again by the freshness of his mind and its instinct for the essentials. We talked a bit, too, about my problems with the international education program, and I mentioned the unsatisfactory talk the President had had with John Rooney. He said that he would do what he could to help if I gave him the word. But I'm not sure that I should. Getting Robert Kennedy's help may not be the best way to get the President's.

❉

At the White House reception for the Diplomatic Corps this evening, the President looked gray with exhaustion.

❉

Some of the people in the Foreign Service have been keeping score: The President is appointing steadily fewer career people to ambassadorial positions. In 1964 the proportion was almost three career people to one from the outside. This year the proportion seems to be moving toward 50-50. Naturally, the Foreign Service isn't happy about it. But there are two sides to that question. The ambassadorial list needs a good representation of outsiders and nonspecialists. Knowing about the world as it looks to people who aren't specialists in foreign policy is a good quality in an ambassador.

However, there is another question that I'm not so sure has two sides. Ever since our difficulties over the UNESCO delegation last fall, and even before that time, the President has been appointing an increasing number of people to quite specialized boards and committees—for example, to choose recipients of academic grants, or to represent the country to international agencies conducting highly technical programs—who don't have the necessary background. My area isn't the only one that has been affected. The White House is exercising control over appointments to an unprecedented degree, and is checking and rechecking personnel decisions that used to be left pretty much to the discretion of Cabinet and sub-Cabinet officers. More and more, the President seems to be naming people known to him personally, and to be resisting the appointment of people he doesn't know.

I remarked to a colleague today, after another long call from the White House about an appointment, that it is almost as though the President thought he was all through and was winding up his Administration by rewarding his friends while he still had the chance. It's all very puzzling. Most of these appointments, though important from the point of view of the work that has to be performed, are to fairly anonymous positions. From a political point of view, they're not plums but peanuts.

May, 1967:

I had a talk with another of the President's assistants today about my leaving. We went over the Vietnam business at length. I like the man enormously, and he made the conversation easier by listening quietly and responding moderately. Not that he granted any of my points; at one or two moments, on the contrary, he showed irritation. But he was, at any rate, listening.

We talked about the Rusk committee as well, and with greater agreement. If I can keep my mind off Vietnam, where I have no influence or jurisdiction, and save such powers of persuasion as I have to promote the idea of a broad new semiautonomous commission to handle educational and cultural affairs, perhaps I can still get something useful done here. One uses up one's capital by getting into domains where one has no official business, and then one doesn't accomplish what one might in one's own domain. But it's become increasingly difficult for me to get other people's minds off Vietnam so they can give some attention to my little neck of the woods, and it's hard for me to do the same thing for myself.

❋

The Bureau of the Budget's representatives and I met with Secretary Rusk today to discuss our preparations for the first meeting of his committee. So far we're not moving along very well, to my mind at least. The focus of the memorandum that is being prepared is not what I should like, and the Secretary, though I think my ideas interest him, doesn't seem in a mood to try anything very radical. The pressures on him mount: not only Vietnam, but the Greek coup, the Arab-Israeli nervousness, the difficulties with the French and his cold war with the Senate Foreign Relations Committee. However, even though the material going to the committee seems to me unsatisfactory, the proposals I have made will also be put before it.

❋

The first meeting of the Rusk committee took place today. Senator Fulbright and Congressmen Mahon and Bow were the only Congressional representatives who were present.

Most of the meeting was taken up with briefing the members of the committee on the variety of government programs in existence and on the ways in which other governments support international activities by private citizens' groups in educational, cultural and philanthropic fields. I was encouraged by the almost unanimous opinion of the private citizens on the committee that it should not perform a mere patch-and-paste job, but should recommend a thorough revision of existing arrangements. They are approaching their task with a sense of fresh and broad possibilities for rationalizing the government's scattered programs of support for educational and cultural affairs, and for redressing the relationship of the government to the educational and cultural community. They have the feeling which I have hoped they would that there is an opportunity here that should be grasped.

Senator Fulbright supported this approach eloquently. He and Rusk did business together in a straightforward manner.

✻

We had our hearing on Education Officers before the Senate Subcommittee on Appropriations. It has been turned down, as I expected, by the House. Senator Pastore was the only member present. The hearing was more careful than the one in the House, but it was also brief. I can't have any hope about the outcome.

✻

Another meeting, involving executive-branch members of the Rusk committee and their aides, took place today to go over the business before the committee. I think the situation is still wide-open, but the concern was expressed that Congress will be in no mood to entertain any new proposals. The question was also raised about how far the President would want to go on this matter. The mood in this town doesn't favor boldness. Still, the mood on the Rusk committee—at least among most of its private members—is more affirmative. Might it not lift people's sights a bit if the committee came in with an imaginative proposal? Congress seems willing to consider a public broadcasting corporation. Why not this?

✻

I had a discussion at the White House today about our difficulties over appointments to committees and commissions. I suggested that it does the Administration no good to have people named to these bodies who aren't qualified, or can't give the time needed, or come with too insistent frequency from Texas. The discussion was amicable, and I think that the next round of appointments will be better. What makes the issue something less than black-and-white is that some of the President's appointments have been first-rate men.

At the Israeli Embassy this evening, the Ambassador and his wife both talked to me with deep concern about events in the Middle East.

*

Wedgwood Benn is in Washington, and we are meeting to discuss the brain drain, the technological gap and other matters. Donald Hornig's office is also involved. Practical proposals were outlined on which we, the British and Western European countries, if they're interested, could take action. But I'm not optimistic. This government is distracted, divided, sullen, in its obsession with Vietnam.

*

An aide of Abba Eban's, who has accompanied him here, called on me today to discuss future educational exchanges with Israel. He said that the situation that had been created by the blockade of the Strait of Tiran was critical, but that he was confident that Israel would somehow see its way through. However, it would be difficult, and there was going to be a great deal of suffering. Eugene Rostow, who has been working on the problem, has outlined to us the efforts to put together a multinational effort to lift the blockade. But it seems to me that this government, overcommitted elsewhere, has precious little freedom of action.

June, 1967:

At the staff meeting with Under Secretary Katzenbach today, the entire time was devoted to the Arab-Israeli confrontation.

Nick remarked ruefully at the end of the hour: "Just to think: I've been waiting for a meeting when there'd be no mention of Vietnam."

✷

The second meeting of the Rusk committee was held today. But before we got going, and again at lunch, conversation was about the Middle East and not our own business. Congressional representation at the meeting was no better than last time.

✷

War broke out between Israel and the Arab countries today. Reports coming in from the Middle East have been terribly confused, but by the end of the day the pattern began to be clear. Arab complaints about American intervention are an unmistakable index to how the fighting is going.

✷

I have been meeting with various members of the Rusk committee. Those I have talked with are almost all in favor of a major reorganization of educational and cultural affairs, involving the establishment of a new semigovernmental commission.

✷

A general meeting was held today of people in the Administration concerned with the business of the Rusk committee. Two rather different philosophies were expressed: one emphasized the idea of exchanges, without direct political purposes; the other emphasized the values of American "voluntarism" and how much we could do to advance the development of other countries by exporting this idea. On the whole, it was younger men, staff assistants and the like, who took the second view. A couple of them have an evangelistic religious background.

The fundamental question, however, is when the Rusk committee will meet again. The Secretary is overwhelmed with problems; the Congressional members aren't attending; and the present mood in the executive branch is to wait awhile in the hope that the mood in Congress will improve. The business of the Rusk committee isn't the only business that is being postponed on this rather doubtful hope.

*

Albert Moseman, who has been the chief educational officer for AID, is leaving. He has said to me that he thinks that education has no future in that organization. Its people and its lines of command have a different orientation.

*

The Glassboro meeting between the President and Kosygin has helped. The President and Bill Fulbright are in contact again. Bill wrote a long letter to the President urging him not to let the chance for a meeting with Kosygin go by, and the President, after calling him late at night to discuss the letter, has been in touch with him several times since. A slight change in mood is discernible in this town.

*

Helen and I were at the White House dinner this evening for the King and Queen of Thailand. While we waited in the East Room for the Johnsons to enter with Their Majesties, a lady I had never met before got into conversation with me. Pointing across the room at one of the President's assistants, she said, as calmly and matter-of-factly as can be imagined, "That man is a traitor."

At dinner, with the Queen between them, the President and Bill Fulbright talked almost continuously. After dinner, Bill and I walked out of the dining room together. Suddenly a large hand grabbed each of us from behind. It was the President. He held Bill in an affectionate embrace with his left arm, while holding my hand tightly in his right. At this point the Queen came up, and the President introduced me to her again. She extended her hand, expecting me to take it, but I couldn't, for the President was still clutching mine.

*

The House Appropriations Subcommittee has cut our budget, but by just the amount of the increase we requested. So we're where we were last year, which—this year—is good.

July, 1967:

I have been in Paris at a small meeting of American university presidents and French rectors. I hope they will create a more formal body allowing them to remain in touch; it could be a useful framework for educational cooperation. Our conversations have dwelt on the French educational reforms and their efforts to create campus-type universities in the Parisian suburbs and the provinces. The Americans discussed their problems in the United States. The parallels struck me as more important than the differences.

*

A high official of this government said to me today that my "lack of interest" in defending the freedom of the Vietnamese might be due to the fact that they weren't "my kind of people." The President, I am told, connects Bill Fulbright's opposition to the war to his conservative stance on civil rights: he seems to suspect that opposition to the war reflects indifference to the fate of dark-skinned people. Is it possible that an inverted desire to avoid racism is present in our Vietnamese policy? Anything, I am beginning to learn, is possible.

*

At the meeting of the Rusk committee today, the debate over the issues finally became sharp. Most of the private members, plus Fulbright, want a new semigovernmental commission with broad authority over a whole variety of international educational, cultural and civic activities. But some of the Administration members have become extremely skittish. They raised warning flags about Congressional attitudes, and one implied to me, in a private conversation during a coffee break, that the President doesn't want anything too ambitious. My own feeling is that we should not be trying to guess his mind, but should give him what we think is our best advice. After that, he can do what he thinks best.

The meeting broke with the understanding that we would canvass the Congressional members who had not been attending before we tried to draw up any final recommendations.

Before and after the meeting, the discussion was about the riots in the cities. "Riots" seems too weak a word for what is happening. And the government seems transfixed—its purposes confused and its authority overdrawn at the bank.

August, 1967:

We are going ahead with a special request to Congress to use zlotys under an agreement with the Poles for English-language training. Ambassador John Gronouski is in town and is spreading the gospel on Capitol Hill. The question, however, is whether he will be able to get people's attention. Newark, Detroit, the other cities, the war, have created an atmosphere of acute depression. But that is all they seem to have created. The lamentations increase; action is nil.

❄

We had our hearings before the Senate Appropriations Subcommittee today. I testified first—it's our last chance—about Education Officers, and began by mentioning the President's international education program. The chairman, Senator McClellan, came down hard on the word "international." He asked if the country hadn't had too much of all this "international" business, and said he thought that a lot of people in Congress were coming to feel that way.

So it went. The hearings on the regular budget got off into a long digression on foreign currencies and why we could or couldn't use them for *all* our programs. There's a foreign-currency hedgehog on the subcommittee staff.

And, of course, just to show my luck, the Administration sent its new and severe tax bill to Congress this very day. That put everybody in a receptive mood toward the CU budget.

※

A group of Columbia College students, serving as summer interns in Congressmen's offices, called on me today, and we had an hour's bull session. They weren't happy; most of them felt they hadn't been given enough to do, and all were anxious about the mood in Washington. But they were refreshingly committed and alert young men. They were eager to know what I did, and when I described my job, they seemed enthralled. They want very much to believe in the government. The whole affair was like old times. It picked up my spirits.

※

Along with a group of sub-Cabinet officials from all the departments, I was called to the White House this morning for a briefing by some of the President's assistants. The need for the tax increase was explained to us, and then we were told about Vietnam. Some high officers of the government, it was said, had reported to the White House that they were constantly being asked, as they went about the country, about the reasons for the war, and had trouble answering. Well, here were the reasons: we were then presented with an argument which, it seemed to me, might have been appropriate—fifty years ago—for high school children. The speech—it was that, not a briefing—dealt with none of the serious questions that have been asked about the war; it simply ignored their existence.

One of the key people in my Department also chimed in with

some arguments that I found astonishing. The most important reason we're in Vietnam, it turns out, is that we're defending Japan! I should think that the most obvious and dominating fact is that our chance to keep on friendly terms with the Japanese depends on our stopping our killing of Asians. As the war goes on, foreign policy people are trotting out speculations misty enough to qualify them as professors of metaphysics.

There wasn't any debate at the meeting; it wasn't that kind of affair. But I resolved to have a talk with my Department colleague.

*

I met late today with my colleague in the Department who had been present at the White House briefing. I had the outline of a memorandum in my pocket; I hoped, whether he agreed with it or not, that he might get some attention for it that I knew I couldn't. But I never took the notes out of my pocket. Our disagreement exploded too fast. The war was absolutely necessary, he said. Only the United States was in a position to keep order in the world, as the British had done a century before.

Our argument went on for two hours.

My colleague, like almost everyone else in the Department, was decent and controlled. Still, my mood was grim when I left his office. I can never quite believe that our present policy on Vietnam rests on the airy optimism and Hegelian assurance about the course of history on which it does rest. And my memorandum was still in my pocket.

September, 1967:

In Honolulu for East-West Center meetings. The Center is no worse off than it was a year or two ago, but it's certainly made no progress either. Everything stands still.

*

The Congressional members of the Rusk committee still haven't been brought together to be briefed.

❋

At the White House today, I got into the Vietnam question again. One man listened, and merely said he thought my perspective might be a little askew. I was an Easterner, a New Yorker. I didn't know the country. But one of his colleagues took a stronger line. He told me, in the tone of a political professional to a political amateur, that the people of the country were behind the President. They would show what they thought in 1968. The election would be the sweepstakes that told the story, and the President was going to win big.

❋

I had lunch with Senator George McGovern today, to outline some of the ideas I've been developing about putting new life into various scattered and neglected activities in the field of foreign affairs, from our food programs to educational exchanges.

The Senator was interested and receptive. At the end of our conversation, he asked me whether the speeches that he and the others gave against the war ever seemed to have any effect in the executive branch. I had to tell him that I was not aware that they did, beyond stiffening people's spines.

❋

Both the Advisory Commission on International Educational and Cultural Affairs and the Board of Foreign Scholarships are growing increasingly restive about the Rusk committee's lack of progress. It isn't enough to say, I have found, that Mr. Rusk and the government have other preoccupations.

❋

After almost two years of talk about coordination, and after shuffling the drafts of Executive Orders uncounted times from

State to HEW to the Bureau of the Budget, it looks as though we're about to begin all over again. Paul Miller met with me in my office, and the problems we discussed were the problems with which we began—except that now we're working on a fourth draft, or is it a fifth or sixth? Each new draft buttons up a problem by unbuttoning an old one. It is interesting that we're still spinning bureaucratic wheels after the issue has become academic. I suppose it's to keep up our spirits. The International Education Act is a dead letter on the books.

October, 1967:

The Senate and the House have agreed on the budget figure for CU first set by the Rooney subcommittee. That's the way it usually works out.

❋

The International Education Act may be a dead letter, but the World Conference on the Crisis in Education opened at Williamsburg today. The idea for it was broached shortly after we began work on the new international education program. Now, two years later, there's not much program left, but the body still moves though the soul has departed. We're holding the conference, and the President will address it. I stayed only for the opening lunch, for I'm to leave for Europe tonight.

14

The Weariness Theory of History

At the end of my first interview with Dean Rusk, just after my nomination as Assistant Secretary, he had asked me, "Have you had any time off recently?" When I said I hadn't, he replied that he thought I'd better get some rest before I came to work.

I had thought he was merely being considerate. I hadn't realized that he had been trying to warn me.

There are ways in which the job of an Assistant Secretary of State isn't as hard as the life of the teacher or writer. As a writer, you thrill with conviction in the morning as the words go down on paper, and snort contemptuously in the evening as you read what some cretin has written a few hours before. As an Assistant Secretary of State, I slept better at night: I came home recognizing that what I had done during the day couldn't be undone, and I didn't spend my nights rewriting. When old friends saw me, they said with surprise that I was looking remarkably well. They shouldn't have been surprised. A steady flow of adrenalin helps one's appearance. And I was no longer leading a double life: I was no longer both the creator and the critic, both the scold and the scolded. My job provided these conveniences for me.

Still, the top floors of the State Department aren't Lotus

Land. In the end, the way of life that I have been describing—its inertia, its sluggish and hypnotic communications system, its alarms, excursions, necessities and happenings, its vastness and disjointedness—all these are felt as physical events. They come down to pains that people feel. They grow tired. Their backs ache, their legs grow stiff and their minds crave problems kept simple and ideas unambitious. The great theories of history, which proclaim the importance of religion, ideas, social classes or technological change, aren't necessarily wrong. But few of them pay sufficient attention to the fact that history, whatever else it may be, is a physiological event.

If one wants to understand why government is what it is and does what it does—or doesn't do what it ought to do—one does well to remember the elementary point that government is work done by human beings; and in the American government it is often overwork. The people who do best in government normally have the constitution and temperament of decathlon champions. They have versatility, endurance and the power to snap back quickly after an exhausting experience. But as in the case of decathlon champions, what pays off for them is the capacity to sustain a high average performance; they don't usually break records in any particular event.

That government service is a decathlon may be suggested by the schedules for a couple of sample days in my own office.

ONE DAY

8:00 A.M.	Meeting with my immediate staff to review the meeting the previous day of the President's Task Force on International Education, and to parcel out follow-up assignments.
8:30	Meeting with staff assistant to go over cables and correspondence that won't wait.
9:00	A quick glance at my day's schedule with my secretary. Two additional appointments squeezed in.

9:05   Telephone call from Science Adviser to President, related to development of better facilities for research in Asian universities. The thought is that the brain drain might be lessened.

9:15   Secretary of State's staff meeting. Around the world in forty-five minutes.

10:00   Meeting with Assistant Secretary of State for Latin American Affairs and Alliance for Progress specialists about educational planning in the OAS.

10:45   Telephone calls, initialing of memoranda, editing of policy statement on exchanges in the arts.

11:15   Meeting in my office with Yugoslav Cabinet Minister and Yugoslav Ambassador.

12:30 P.M.   Lunch with Senator Fulbright, to tell him about the Administration's new initiatives in international education.

2:00   Back to office. Meeting with CU's Director of African Programs canceled; meeting with my press officer substituted: preparation of special statement for newspapers to clear up misunderstanding about cultural exchanges with Soviet Union. Clearance requested from Bureau of European Affairs and Bureau of Public Affairs.

2:30   Conference with counsel of the Kennedy Center, to discuss problems before the Executive Committee of the Trustees.

3:00   Meeting with members of my staff to be briefed on the meeting the next day of the Government Advisory Committee on Books and Library Programs, related to needs for U.S. textbooks abroad.

3:30   Meeting with our Ambassador to Ghana: the problem, Nkrumah.

4:00   Correspondence and urgent telephone calls postponed; two alternative statements on Soviet exchanges received from Bureau of European Affairs and Bureau of Public Affairs. Arguments heard, telephone calls made to each Bureau. Special troubleshooter assigned to work out or obscure the disagreements.

4:30   Meeting with Assistant Secretary for International Organizations to discuss the U.S. position in the coming vote on the countries that should be represented on the UNESCO Executive Board.

5:00   Meeting with representatives of Bureaus of European Affairs and Public Affairs. One sentence and two commas deleted from the joint statement that has been worked out since 4:00 o'clock. Issue settled.

5:30   Meeting with the president of an American university in the Middle East, which needs money.

5:45   Dictation of letters; call to Congressman replying to call he had put in to me; call from Internal Revenue Service about tax status of visiting foreign scholars.

6:10   Call from White House to ask my reaction to a statement that has been prepared for announcement by the President; I suggest that one sentence and two commas be inserted.

6:30   Reception at the Iraqi Embassy for Iraqi Prime Minister and Foreign Minister.

8:00   Dinner at my home: two of my colleagues from CU, an Under Secretary from HEW, an editorial writer from the Washington *Post*, and wives.

11:15   Help my wife with the dishes. The maid engaged for the evening didn't show.

ANOTHER DAY
8:00 A.M.   Meeting with CU deputies and budget officers to discuss the budget presentation for the Bureau.

8:30   Meeting with chairman of Board of Foreign Scholarships, which selects grantees under the Fulbright program.

9:00   Staff assistant: urgent memoranda and cables.

9:15   Discussion of day's schedule with my secretary. She reluctantly agrees to add an appointment.

9:30   Attend meeting of the Board of Foreign Scholarships.

10:00   Leave meeting to return to my office; receive formal protest from Ambassador from ———, complaining about public statements made in his country by the American Cultural Affairs Officer; promise to look into the facts; the meeting ends on an amicable note.

10:20   Order an investigation of the facts; call USIA, which employs the man in question, to discuss the problem. They are sure the facts are wrong.

10:30   Conference by telephone with Commissioner of Education, related to training programs for foreign teachers in this country.

10:40   Emergency meeting with officer in CU in charge of visa problems to discuss urgent case.

10:45   Meeting with Peace Corps representatives to discuss availability of Peace Corps Volunteers for new English-language teaching assignments abroad.

11:00   Meeting with newly appointed American Ambassador to Pakistan to discuss educational and cultural relations with that country.

11:30   Back to meeting of Board of Foreign Scholarships.

12:30 P.M. Hurried meeting with Budget Office on seventh floor to say that there must be some mistake about the figure which, I have just heard, has been set for my Bureau.

1:00   Lunch in State Department Dining Room with visiting Minister of Education and the ambassador from his country. Good talk, a warm exchange of toasts, mediocre wine.

2:30   Meeting with members of staff to discuss next day's meeting of Federal Inter-Agency Council on International Educational and Cultural Affairs.

3:00   Call to Bureau of the Budget to discuss CU budget problems; correspondence.

3:30   Discussion of personnel matters in Bureau with aides.

3:50   Unscheduled interruption: prominent American choreographer, who accompanied modern dance company in Soviet Union, feels that she was snubbed there, and has returned threatening to damn the whole exchange program in a statement to the newspapers tomorrow; I call people who know her, explaining the larger issues and expressing my hope that she will postpone making her statement until she has more time to think about it.

4:15   Receive representatives of 4-H clubs in my office; formal presentation of paperweight to me. It seems small. Does 4-H *know* the weight of papers?

4:30   Meeting with presidents of American Council of Learned Societies, Social Science Research Council, National Academy of Sciences and American Council on Education.

5:30   Brief speech at reception for visiting Japanese newspapermen.

6:00   Meeting at White House to discuss policy on communications satellites.

7:15   Back in my office for last-minute rerun of issues to be discussed at my appearance before House Immigration Subcommittee the next morning, particularly the problem of foreign doctors resident in the U.S.

8:00   Dinner at the ——— Embassy. During dinner, discussion with the Ambassador's wife, on my left, of the marijuana cult among students; discussion with the lady on my right of I can't remember what. After dinner, a brief *tête-à-tête* with the Ambassador about his government's developing plans to make financial contributions to Fulbright program.

11:10   On the dot, departure home.

11:30   Have I read that memorandum for tomorrow's meeting? I have not. Get to work.

Compared with the schedules of others at my level in the Department, these may well have been easy days. They offer no examples of the long meetings that go on until the early hours of the morning to deal with crises that come up almost each week in Berlin or Cyprus, in Yemen or Argentina or Pakistan. Unlike most of my colleagues, I was only a part-time fireman, and my life was less subject than theirs to disruption. As for the Secretary of State, an act of unusual imagination is needed to grasp the physical punishment that goes with his position. Each September, when the United Nations General Assembly met in New York, Dean Rusk, in a period of about two weeks, conferred with the heads of over a hundred foreign delegations. And yet this was probably among his easier seasons of the year. During these two weeks, at least, he could usually tell what was coming.

If a certain quality of balkiness, even of condescension, sometimes shows itself in the attitudes of State Department people toward academic critics and editorial writers, or toward Congressmen, Senators and bright young men in the White House who generate new ideas, this is to be partly explained, I suspect, by such physical facts. I saw Dean Rusk return to his office one day after a stormy six-hour session with the Senate Foreign

Relations Committee. He stopped at the door to his office to answer a pressing question I had to ask him about a very different matter, turned to another Assistant Secretary to do the same, and then disappeared into his office, followed by an assistant with a file of cables in his hand that was three inches thick. The assistant emerged in a moment, and I could see the Secretary, through the open door, his jacket off, picking up the first cable on the pile and looking at it with the slightly skeptical expression of a professional buyer inspecting a sample. The Secretary's assistant closed the door, turned to my colleague and me, and swept his hand in a weary gesture in the general direction of Capitol Hill. "They're a bunch of damned dilettantes," he said.

It isn't the mere pace of events that distinguishes a job in the upper echelons of the government. What also distinguishes it is the variety of responsibilities that goes into it.

In my position, to offer it again as an example, I had at least six discriminable kinds of duty to perform. Each required a special kind of knowledge and action; each required, indeed, a different manner and tone of voice. I was in charge, as director of CU's grant-making activities, of what was in effect a large educational foundation, working through an elaborate system of committees and commissions in the United States and abroad; I was an adviser in the development of national policy in one major area of foreign relations; I was regularly consulted by the White House and HEW on domestic educational policies that had international implications, and, by other agencies, on matters related to the arts, sciences, humanities and communications; I served as diplomat, negotiator and principal representative of the government in its international educational and cultural relations; I acted as the principal coordinator, the source of "policy guidance and leadership," for the activities of all federal departments and agencies touching on international education or cultural relations; and I was a member of governing boards or coordinating councils responsible for such government enterprises as the National Endowment for the Arts, the National Endowment for the Humanities, and the Kennedy Center.

Simply to list the committees and commissions with which I was officially required to meet may be an eye-opener about the nature of government service:

The United States Advisory Commission on International Educational and Cultural Affairs

The Federal Inter-Agency Council on International Educational and Cultural Affairs

The Board of Foreign Scholarships

The United States Advisory Commission on UNESCO

The United States Advisory Committee on the Arts

The Federal Council on the Arts and Humanities

The Federal Inter-Agency Council on Education

The Government Advisory Committee on International Book and Library Programs

The Inter-Agency Committee on International Book and Library Programs

The Executive Committee of the John F. Kennedy Center for the Performing Arts

The National Review Board of the East-West Center for Technical and Cultural Interchange

The Committee on American Schools Overseas

The total is twelve. Each met at intervals ranging from six weeks to three months, making sixty or seventy meetings a year. And from time to time I met with other groups, like the Federal Council on Science and Technology and the President's Advisory Committee on Foreign Aid. In addition, there were, of course, *ad hoc* committees, created to deal with special problems. I was always on at least three or four of these. The simple problem of avoiding schedule conflicts among so many meetings turned out to be insoluble. Which meeting does one attend? That itself is a policy decision, a determination of priorities. And one must make this determination in a context in which one is also on call by the Congress and the press, in which one must travel and make speeches, and in which, at eight on a Wednesday evening, when one is just preparing to leave one's office, a cable will come in marked "urgent" that has been sent by an ambassador halfway around the world who has just arrived, bright and bushy-tailed, in his office on Thursday morning, and wants to know why those characters in Washington always seem to be so slow.

I would be giving a wholly false impression if I seem to be complaining. On the contrary, I found the experience exhilarating. It was like a football game in which, during the time-outs, the players engage in a snappy game of tennis, shift to ice hockey, and then, after the final whistle blows and the crowd goes off to the cocktail parties, settle down to a crew race topped off by a series of wind sprints. One isn't bored. But one doesn't give the attention to each problem which, taken by itself, it may deserve.

I thought, for example, that the Kennedy Center was an important venture. It could do much, both practically and symbolically, to raise American tastes and aspirations in the arts, and it could also do something, I believed, to improve the quality of American politics and government. Washington needs another source of illumination, passion and amusement besides the goings-on at the White House and the Congress. It seemed to me that I ought to use what influence I had to prevent the Center from becoming only a pretentious building where the famous and the fashionable came to show themselves off. But I wasn't able to do a quarter of what I wished with regard to the Center. I attended meetings when I could, specifically delegated one of my assistants to devote a portion of his time to it, and called colleagues on the Center's Executive Committee every couple of months to discuss its future. But I couldn't do the one essential thing, which was to follow up steadily on important suggestions. I simply had too many other things to do.

Thus government goes slack. It depends on people near the top to push ideas and programs through, but these people are unable to give to all these ideas and programs the required push. There are sometimes some fairly simply explanations of why initiatives fall flat in government: the man you need to reach at a critical moment is out of his office when you call; the man to whom you are talking, and whose attention you need, has another appointment bearing down on him in five minutes; the two or three people whose help will put an idea over are simply overcommitted, overextended, short on time, short on desire.

Nor is it just that they, and you, and the others who must pull together are moving at a furious pace and trying to manage myriad problems. The tax a government position exacts is emotional as well as physical. It requires an ability to shift perspectives, to move precipitately from one scheme of values to another, to focus on what is immediately at hand without letting the day or week or month that lies ahead of you get you down.

One kind of tempo, mood and idiom is needed to talk to a visiting Minister of Education about his country's requirements for secondary-school teachers; another tempo and mood, and a radical change in idiom, are needed, immediately afterward, to discuss the problem of Radcliffe girls with an angry Congressman on the telephone. He has met a young lady from Radcliffe on a ship in the Caribbean, and she has told him that she was a Fulbright grantee traveling to Argentina to learn to dance the tango. He wants to know what the hell's going on in this government, and you have to suggest to him, without quite putting it into words, that perhaps the damsel had been pulling his leg. Then you go back to your next appointment, which requires you to determine the relative merits of spending a million dollars to support tours for orchestras as against attendance by scholars at international meetings.

To move without time to think from one such universe of discourse to another takes presence of mind, self-discipline and a tough nervous system. And after a while the probabilities mount that those who have learned to cope with such requirements for survival will begin to show the symptoms men usually show when they have been subjected to the combination of too many stimuli and too little sleep—dogged persistence on an established course, inability to bring distant objects into focus, progressive loss of the capacity to detect fundamental changes in the environment. That men can be subjected to the pressures of the present method of doing business in the American government and can still go on being flexible and responsive is a bad bet. But it is the bet on which we now run the American government.

It is tempting to dismiss the weariness problem by saying that it was a special characteristic of the Administration in which I served. Undoubtedly, it was an unusual Administration in this respect. A frenetic pressure, a sense that there was no tomorrow, emanated steadily from the White House. It never slacked off until the summer of 1967, when the war and the condition of the cities produced a mood of melancholy fatalism. President Johnson attempted too much in too many different areas, and he wore people out—his friends even more than his enemies. Nevertheless, the weariness theory applies to a considerable extent, I suspect, to any American Administration that is trying to do more than mark time.

A sensible President, and a sensible nation, would demand that their highest officials take regular vacations. And unless there are exceptionally urgent reasons for officials to stay in their posts, most of them should get out after four or five years. If there were no other reason than this for elections, it would be quite enough. Elections are a regimen that allow governments to get a second wind. But even elections touch only the surface of the problem. Our political structures are now so organized that weariness is their constant product. Too many problems come home to Washington to roost. The United States is suffering from the political disease that someone has identified as apoplexy at the center and anemia at the extremities.

But the causes of weariness in government go beyond governmental structures and the pace of government business. They are moral and psychological. It is taxing to stand on the outside, to see public events taking a melancholy course and to feel that you can do nothing about it. But one is subject to a greater and subtler kind of toll when one is on the inside. When a man joins a government, he has to pay his dues. He has to become, to some extent, a believer. And his weariness chart is usually a pretty good index to what is happening to his beliefs.

Whether a man is commenting on events or making practical decisions about them, he is involved in making predictions about the direction in which events are tending and the likely consequences of doing this or doing that. And both the commentator on the outside and the actor on the inside will realize, if they are reasonable, that social and political affairs are full of accidents and unpredictable contingencies, and that when one looks ahead to the future more than one possibility exists. Yet there is a difference between the man who thinks he might have some leverage on events and the man who is looking at them as an outside observer. The man on the inside is involved in an act of faith.

In 1965, when he was urging me to come into the government, Senator Fulbright was already concerned about the war in Vietnam, although he had not spoken out publicly. He said that he thought that a quiet behind-the-scenes effort to persuade the President to try a different course was likely to have better results than a public attack upon the Administration's policy. And in support of this approach, he produced a number of general propositions about the nature of Washington politics and the character of the existing Administration. All of these had considerable truth to them. But there were other propositions, equally persuasive, that he might also have produced and that would have led to the reverse conclusion. Why, then, did he choose the propositions that he did? Was he engaged in dispassionate analysis of the relative probabilities, or was he indulging in wishful thinking?

The answer is that the line can't be drawn that neatly. The alternatives posed by these questions aren't the pertinent alternatives. He was predicting *and* determining where to put his efforts, making a judgment *and* hoping against hope. He thought that he had a better chance to make his point if he didn't cause public commotion, and he thought it would be better all around if this course worked. And when I say, "He thought," I do not mean that he necessarily would have put it in these words. I describe a mood, a willingness to take a chance because it is the right chance to take, and not an act of conscious calculation.

After I entered the government, I found dozens of other individuals similarly hoping against hope. Vietnam was not the only issue, and the phenomenon, I think, is not a phenomenon special to any particular Administration. It is a governmental state of mind. In fact, it is not a phenomenon of government as such; it is a phenomenon of involvement, of engagement, in any field. It characterizes the citizen who works for a political candidate against whom the odds are heavy, the professor who calls for reason and moderation in the middle of a campus demonstration, the surgeon who recommends an operation against the long chance that it will succeed.

We are dealing with what William James called "the will to believe." A man in the grandstand at the races can study the dope sheet and decide that Gigolo is a good three-to-one bet against Ballet Dancer. But the jockey who is riding Ballet Dancer, though he may know the odds, has to think or hope, has to will-and-believe, that Ballet Dancer has a good chance, or else he won't ride the horse seriously. The same is true in government. A sensible man in government knows that he will accomplish much less than he wants and will probably pay more for these accomplishments than he ever realizes in advance. But a man who does not want to cash in his chips—who does not want to say that his cause is finished—goes on hoping.

He goes on hoping, usually, longer than those who have not

made the investment he has in the government. And the deepest kind of weariness comes when that investment no longer yields interest. People on the outside regularly misunderstand why someone inside a government has decided to leave. They look for something specific; they ask what changed the man's mind and made him finally see the light. The morning after the press carried the news of my resignation, I received a telegram from a group of about twenty clergymen and students at Cornell, telling me that they were praying for me in my hour of anguish. Well, it was not at all an enjoyable experience, but I hadn't been living through the dark night of the soul. I had merely taken a decision that I had long since known I would probably have to take, before the coming of the campaign year of 1968, if things kept going along the same downward path. So far as my hopes of accomplishing anything were concerned, I had simply come to the end of the path.

It is true that people often leave an Administration over one specific issue. More often, however, if the people I have known are a fair sample, they leave over an accumulation of things. And they do not make the decision in the flush of new knowledge or conviction. The moral life cannot be cut to the need of melodramatic novelists or evangelistic political commentators for sharp distinctions and climactic moments. For men in the middle of the action, where the chance to make even a small difference is a big chance, the moral life is not usually a series of agonies of conversion. They experience quite enough agony in their day-to-day effort to keep their tempers and their balance. And when they leave, it is usually simply because they have grown tired and have had enough. The outsider asks, "What made you decide to leave, what specific thing?" It is a question that comes out of a different world of thought and action. All the insider can say is that the decision didn't feel like a sharp decision. It didn't follow a *crise de conscience*. All that had happened was that his faith and hope, if not his charity, were used up. He thought that perhaps he could do more good, and recover his hope, on the outside.

15

Disengagement:
Excerpts from a Log

October, 1967:

In Madrid, Ambassador Duke brought together for dinner at the embassy this evening a lively group of people. Most of them expected, and seemed prepared to accept, considerable changes in Spain. Over the brandy and cigars the men discussed two subjects: (1) the modernization of the Spanish economy; (2) the stealing of Columbus Day in the United States by the Italians. Didn't we Americans remember that Spaniards had sponsored the voyage? Shouldn't they have a piece of the credit too? One man said Columbus couldn't even speak Italian, that he came from a Spanish family that had migrated to Genoa.

❋

On the plane to Stockholm, I've read a copy of *Le Monde*, containing a comment on the speech by President Johnson at Williamsburg, in which he returned to the themes of the Smithsonian Address. It may be supposed, says *Le Monde*, that when the American President speaks of international education, he has in mind the destruction of schools in Vietnam and the salubrious instructional effects of bombs.

❋

In Stockholm, we're the guests of the Swedish Institute, which is in charge of Sweden's cultural activities abroad. The status and programs of the Institute, a semiprivate organization supported mainly by government, are being re-examined by a Royal Commission. The officials of the Institute and members of the Commission have been meeting with me to pick my brains. I've given a lecture under their auspices and had some lively conversations. I'm a bit amused. The recommendations which are being drawn up by the Commission make use of the book I published in 1966 on educational and cultural affairs. My ideas appear to have more influence in Stockholm than in Washington.

I've learned, yet once again, that there's no magic cure for the basic problem related to government-supported cultural activities. It exists no matter what the government or country. The Swedish Institute is a good model for the kind of organization that I wish the Rusk committee would recommend, but its officials face the same problem I do at home. Sweden's urgent interest, in international affairs, is to improve its export trade, and the pressure has been put on the Institute to develop programs more directly related to that purpose.

In the United States the need to insulate the cultural programs from the grosser pressures for "evidence of effectiveness" —read: quick political or economic benefits—is recognized in the Fulbright-Hays Law, which puts the power to make academic grants in the hands of a board composed mainly of private citizens, and which surrounds the Assistant Secretary with a network of advisory groups of laymen. Sweden goes further and does better: its government votes the money to an organization with a private board of directors, so that the program is further removed from the bureaucracy and Parliament. But, in the end, the man at the top of a governmentally supported organization in charge of cultural affairs is going to have to have a stiff spine. If he doesn't, the organization's integrity will be eroded. All that can be done is to help him by cutting the connection of the organization with a foreign ministry or information service. This leads to fewer misconceptions of his function.

*

I lunched today with Mr. Pälme, the Minister of Education, who is said to be the rising star in the Swedish government. He is also said to be extremely anti-American, and something of an idol to many of the younger people in the country. I could understand why when I met him. He is young, handsome, astute and impatient to get on with Sweden's social reforms.

We had an agreeable lunch, and Pälme felt free to speak frankly to me over coffee afterward. He had spent some time, it turned out, as a student at Kenyon College, in Ohio. He knew he was thought to be anti-American, he said, but the fact was that he had liked the country very much. He was opposed to American *policies*, not to Americans. Then he brought up the CIA. It had infiltrated an international youth organization in Europe in which he had been active, taking advantage of his trustingness and of many other young people's. And when the facts were discovered and publicized, he had been seriously embarrassed. What was he to think, from that time on, about dealing with the American government?

I repeated the story to people at our embassy later. Ah, yes, they said, he's very anti-American, of course.

*

In Paris, to confer with our mission to UNESCO, and to meet with members of its Executive Board. Not much is being said any more about new American initiatives in international education, and I kept away from the subject.

*

Back in Washington. The city seems shaken by the students' march on the Pentagon. Not that anybody's views on Vietnam appear to have been changed; on the contrary, those I've spoken with are shaking their heads over "the crazy kids."

In the White House the main reaction, not only to the demonstration but to the criticism in Congress and the country, is that the President is a victim of quite unjust attack. His Lincolnian fortitude is constantly praised. The phrase most frequently used to describe his critics is "self-righteous."

*

The Rusk committee stands just where it did when I left. The majority wants to recommend an ambitious reform, the minority is hesitant, and most of the Congressional members are indifferent to the whole thing.

*

I've had a final talk with one of the President's assistants, to tell him that I was going ahead with my plan to resign, and would set it for the end of the year. Assuming that no miracle happens to make me change my plan, I'll give the usual six weeks' notice in November. But I haven't talked with Secretary Rusk yet; it's been impossible to arrange an appointment with him.

The conversation at the White House led, naturally enough, into a discussion of the Vietnam question yet once again. My friend and I went at it pretty hard. I think he's tortured about the war, though he didn't say so. At any rate, he grew more impatient with me than he had in the past.

When I do think coolly about my leaving, I recognize that the question isn't really whether I am right to stay but whether I'm right to go. The program I've been supervising will lose a defender, the Bureau will suffer, the idea for the new foundation will be doomed, and the few weak words I've been able to speak against Vietnam to people close to the President won't be spoken. Perhaps if I stayed I could slow down the retreat from the purposes expressed in the Smithsonian Address.

But the probability is that there is going to be a further retreat, and I won't be able to do anything about it. I'll merely be fronting for a fraud. And I've spoken now to at least a dozen men who have quick access to the President, saying what I think about Vietnam. Despite the sympathy with which some of them have listened, it's been like talking in the void.

November, 1967:

I've been trying to see the Secretary. Finally, just as I was on my way to a reception at 5:30 today, the message came that he would be able to see me at 7:00. I returned to my office around 6:45 and was told that he was delayed. While I was waiting, a telegram was brought to me from some twenty Swarthmore teachers and students. I'm to give a talk there to-morrow on "The Moral Responsibilities of Intellectuals." The telegram said that if I were to talk on anything but Vietnam, I would be guilty of "irrelevance."

I called Courtney Smith, Swarthmore's President, and told him that, as Assistant Secretary for Cultural Affairs, it had been my policy to separate cultural affairs sharply from the political aspects of foreign policy and to say nothing in public about Vietnam, NATO or any other strictly political issue. I suggested to him that I would be happy to speak personally to the teachers and students who had sent the telegram and try to explain the situation to them. He agreed.

While I was speaking to him, Lillian Lovitz entered to tell me the Secretary was now free to see me. I went up to find him alone in his office, slogging through papers. We talked a bit about the Rusk committee and the delay attending its work, and then I told him that I was going to resign. "I don't like this war," I said. "Do you think anybody likes it?" he answered.

We talked for over two hours, going over all the options. I pulled no punches and said what I thought. And I have never had a more reasonable or temperate conversation about the war with any man. But he didn't budge an inch and didn't grant me a point. And while he spoke with more passion than he shows in public, he didn't say anything to me that he doesn't say in public.

I came home close to midnight feeling depleted. "If only the man were a son of a bitch," I said to Helen, "it would all have been much easier to take."

The worst part of this job is that one has to live with divided feelings. I've worked with disciplined and enduring men, who've taken terrible blows for what they believe; respecting them, I've still thought them very wrong and responsible for a tragic disaster. How does one explain this to the outsider? But one can't live with such feelings indefinitely. I'm glad I've been able to sustain them as long as I have. They go with public life, I suspect, even in easier times.

*

At Swarthmore this morning, I talked with some of the young men and women who had sent the telegram; they seemed somewhat less agitated when we had finished.

The speech went well. After saying that I would not alter the subject on which the college community, in accordance with its regular procedures, had invited me to speak, I went on to point out that my subject was relevant to the debate over Vietnam. It was, in fact, basic: What are the rules that should govern debate and responsible action on any issue of passionate concern? The students were very quiet as they listened, and their applause, when I had finished, went beyond mere politeness.

Afterward, I met in a large room with a great crowd of students—perhaps two hundred or more—who sat or stood in a circle around me. We talked about two kinds of politics: one whose focus is on the day-after-tomorrow, a politics of theater, of demonstration, of purification, which, at its best, changes men's sensibilities, their acceptance of things they have regarded as unavoidable; the second a politics that starts-from-now, with the alternatives available and tries to make our wait for salvation a little more endurable. I wasn't surprised at these students' indignation over the state of things. What heartened me was their curiosity, their eagerness to argue and to listen, their willingness to confront ideas and experience, and the passionate desire of most of them, despite all, to go on believing in the political process.

*

I sent in my formal resignation today. Lillian Lovitz at first refused to type it.

*

The Rusk committee still percolates weakly. Another meeting with the Secretary and people from the Bureau of the Budget was held today, at which it was agreed that an effort would be made to bring the Congressional members of the committee together for a briefing.

*

The news suddenly broke today about my resignation. It caught me by surprise, since the President hasn't yet accepted it. Late this afternoon, the press office of the Department called me to say that a story was shortly going to break that I was resigning and that Vietnam was the reason. Would I deny it? It was followed by other calls, longer in length and more heated, and from people steadily higher in the hierarchy. Their import was much the same: Vietnam policy wasn't in my jurisdiction, I had never been consulted about it, and I could hardly say that it had been pursued over my objections. How then could I let the story stand that I was resigning because of it? I didn't want to elevate my importance as a Vietnam dissenter, for it was minuscule, but I couldn't deny a true story—that I disagreed with Vietnam policy, felt its damaging effects in my area, and wouldn't now be leaving except for these reasons. The final call—an angry one—came from the White House late in the evening, after I'd finally gotten home.

One of the reporters who called me gave me some news. "So you're lining up with McNamara, are you?" he asked. I said I didn't follow. "McNamara's leaving in a few months," he said. "The news just leaked, along with the news about you. You don't mean to say you didn't know?"

Of course, I did mean to say just that.

*

I left for Honolulu this morning, rather pleased to be away from my Washington phone after all the calls last night. But when I arrived in Honolulu, the reporters were out in full force. I confined myself to saying what was on the top of my mind— that, after working for two and a half years with people I respected, and after having gone through a number of adventures with them, it was hard to leave without personal regret.

December, 1967:

A group of Congressmen had a small farewell party for me. They're impressive fellows. I felt a little like Huck Finn attending his own funeral.

The number of strong and devoted men in Congress is an arresting but somewhat saddening fact. The men with whom I met today are young. They're going to have to put in considerable time before they acquire the seniority that will give them some genuine power. Some of them will lose their seats before that happens; a number of them, I suspect, will become discouraged and leave politics. We pay a terrible price for the Congressional committee system.

*

There was an awards ceremony today in the Department auditorium, where I sat on the platform along with the Secretary and other officials. Before the ceremony, we gathered in a room backstage. I can't say that I was actively ignored, but there was an area of empty space around me. Dean Rusk, over at the other end of the room, saw me over the heads of the people surrounding him and came over to keep me company. He said that he had just had a meeting with a number of the Congressional members of the Rusk committee. The report was that they weren't interested in doing very much and had given the impression that the meeting was an interruption in other, more important business.

*

The atmosphere in this town is eerie. Now that I'm leaving, I'm perhaps more aware of it than ever. Some of the Cabinet members with whom I've spoken seem sunk in melancholia, and all sorts of other people, from Assistant Secretaries to messengers from the mail room, talk as though they feel dazed by the condition of the government.

"Dazed" is the word. It's a government that acts as though it has been overcome by History. Those who have made the decisions, who had the chance repeatedly to reconsider, have the feeling now that they weren't decisions but duties imposed by external events. The President and his advisers were formed by the traumatic experiences of Munich and Korea. Under the influence of these mistaken analogies, under the pressures of ego and conscience, of one investment in blood piled on another, of criticism that has stiffened them against considering alternatives, these policies have taken on a life of their own. They aren't things to be changed but to be endured. Everything in the President's attitude whenever I have seen him—his sagging shoulders, his references to Lincoln—suggests that he thinks of himself as the victim of a destiny he hasn't chosen but won't dodge.

The effects have been hypnotic. If I were to judge only from what high officials have said to me, and have been saying to the country, I would have no reason to suspect that there is any connection between the trouble in our cities and the trouble with our foreign policy. I wouldn't know that the war in Vietnam has sickened most of the people abroad whose friendship we need, or that it is making our universities ungovernable and reducing a generation of young Americans to rage and despair. I wouldn't even suspect that there was a case to be made for stopping the bombing of North Vietnam, or for reducing it. Those who have such ideas are unprofessional, irresponsible, eccentric. If we stop the bombing or reduce it, I've been told, we would simply reduce the one incentive the North Vietnamese have to negotiate.

Is it possible that those with whom I've discussed these propositions, and who have taken such views, really think differently? I suppose one or two do. But the answers most of them have given me in private are the same as those they've given in public. In private they merely speak with a more obvious and passionate sincerity. In any case, whatever they're thinking behind their official masks, they've made their decisions on the basis of these official propositions. The country hasn't been suffering from a "credibility gap" but from an "incredibility gap." People can't believe that the President and the Secretary of State really believe what they say. But they do.

✳

My last day in the office. Dean Rusk's assistant called to say that the Secretary hoped I could have a drink with him in the afternoon. I thanked him, but said I had to get home to help move my family, and, besides, another conversation like our last would about do me in.

We moved out of the apartment to a motel and leave tomorrow.

✳

Helen drove the car. I slept almost all the way.

16

The Unruliness of Men

At the end of 1967, education was in crisis, the cities were in turmoil, and funds were being cut back for most of the programs which the Administration had initiated. During the course of two and a half years I had watched from the inside while an American Administration, rich in promise and enjoying extraordinary support from the people, had stubbornly, obsessively, destroyed its promise and dissolved its power.

The byword of the Johnson Administration, when I entered it, was "cost-benefit analysis." It was hoped that this method of carefully weighing alternatives by measuring their costs against their projected benefits might introduce more rationality not only into the planning of military weaponry but into decision-making throughout the government. Yet this was the Administration which made decisions, not once but repeatedly, that took the country ever more deeply into a war which had mounting costs and indiscernible benefits. When President Johnson took office, he said that he hoped, above all, to bring unity and consensus to the country. In March, 1968, he announced that he would not run for re-election because he had become the symbol of division.

It was as though the government in which I had served had been caught in a predestined engagement with disaster. And what was most disturbing, as I looked back, was that the causes seemed to go beyond the accidents of particular personalities and a particular Administration. How could the government, with all the resources at its disposal, with all the money it spends to obtain information, with all the people it keeps busy forecasting events and making plans—how could it lose its sense of direction and its touch on reality? What I had seen was the immense momentum of the government machinery itself, the vast pressure of the government's way of doing things, helping to support and reinforce the Administration's trancelike movement downhill.

In this sense, the story was only incidentally—almost coincidentally—the story of one particular Administration. It was a story that might be true, though perhaps to a lesser extent, of any Administration. Admittedly, part of the answer to why national policy followed the course that it did between 1964 and 1968 lay in the character of President Johnson and his chief advisers. Special premiums were paid for briefs in defense of existing policies. But these quirks of personality and political style might have been modified and counterbalanced if the government did not have more permanent characteristics of its own. For all the criticism that went on inside it, for all its cross-currents, it somehow managed, in the end, to thwart change and conserve illusions.

If there was any central theme in my experience in the government, this was it—the strange separateness of the government, the sense it gives, at the center of the action, of being somehow disengaged. There were other themes as well—the birth and death of a new venture in foreign policy, the fall of an Administration that lost itself in a blind obsession with a war in which the country had no business. But again and again I had been struck by a phenomenon for which I was only half-prepared—the way the government has of keeping its eye on its own star, of hearing only the music it wants to hear. It has bouts of somnambulism, in which, like a sleepwalker, it seems capable of receiving signals only from within. It proves itself better at lulling itself with dubious abstractions—"commitments," "deterrence," "world leadership"—than at looking at facts like human grief, national doubt or the isolation of the United States from world opinion.

Obviously, the government isn't invariably out of touch with the outside world. Books can be written about all the ways in which it is responsive and, for our sins, a great many such books have been written. The government is surrounded by instruments of all sorts intended to interrupt its waking dream —electoral processes, an opposition party, a separate Congress, a rambunctious press, a scholarly community with no deficiency of mavericks, a nation full of pushers and organizers and demonstrators. Sometimes the noise gets through. Lyndon Johnson, after all, did finally decide that he had had it. Yet the mystery, given all the immense precautions that are taken in our society to keep the government responsive, is why it so often remains lost in its own dream of reality. No government is ever more than partially responsive; every government is able to hear some people better than others. But the curious fact about the American government recently has been its distance from, its slow reaction time to, massive movements of sentiment and opinion. It seems to be listening mainly to itself.

Are they right, then, those who say that the government is unsalvageable? In part, its faults, I believe, are due to its encrusted manners and mores. If people on the inside become more aware of them, if people on the outside keep the heat on, and if there is enough circulation of fresh people into the government and tired people out of it, these conventions can be modified to some extent. And there are also things that can be done to change some of the broader conditions that cut the government off from the world outside.

Our political parties, as I believe others have noticed besides myself, are not sufficiently accessible to new men and new ideas. They are better at guarding memories of past glories or old grudges than at registering emerging sentiments and reacting to existing facts. This can be changed, and it is a process which the Democrats, one hopes, have begun. But behind that problem—the problem of making the parties more responsive— lies the deeper problem of being able to take the parties' assertions of policy seriously, of being able to hold them responsible, as parties, for what they do or do not do. And this takes us to the phenomenon of the Congressional committee system.

It is a system that cuts loose the most powerful men in Congress from the control of the parties and tends to put the parties in their control. And it gives this power to men few of whom speak for broadly representative constituencies. They are the men who come, by and large, from the safe states and districts, from the economic and cultural islands of the country. This system by which Congress organizes itself into satrapies is probably the largest single reason for the unresponsiveness of the legislature and the disjointedness of our government. Yet nothing in our Constitution requires Congress to be organized as it is.

Congress, considered as a group of individuals, is fairly representative of the country. Considered as a collection of committees—which is how it functions—it is closer to gerontocracy than democracy, and it gives far more than one-man-one-vote to the people in the districts from which the committee chairmen come. Major improvements in the behavior of both the executive and the legislative branches could be produced, I venture to think, if the seniority system for selecting committee chairmen were replaced by a system in which the Majority Leaders in the two chambers named the chairmen and members of standing committees at each session of Congress. I am aware that informed students of this subject hold many different views and that this proposal raises thorny issues. Certainly, it has risks as well as merits. One will lose good men as well as bad as committee chairmen. But the transcendent issues of party responsibility and effective participation by the Congress in the formation of policy are involved in the too-long-postponed question of Congressional reorganization.

That is a place to begin. More broadly still, we need to ask whether a government in Washington is not too vast in scale, too crowded, too remote, to be either accessible or effective. Men are simply too secluded in Washington and have too much to do to be able to keep their ears open or their responses flexible. Between the state governments, whose jurisdictions are increasingly artificial, and the federal government, whose jurisdiction is so large and abstract, there is a vacuum in governmental power.

New forms of regional government are required to permit the creation of a modernized federal system that would remove from Washington some portion of the activities that now go on there and would leave greater room for initiative and variety to different areas of the country. To relieve the pressure on the center, new structures are needed, large enough to pull together the forces that should be concerted and close enough to the citizenry to be more easily reached. The federal government cannot abandon its responsibility to ensure common standards of education, welfare or human rights, to regulate the national economy, or to give special help to places and people in the country that need it. But it can carry on more of these enterprises indirectly, standing behind them but standing back from them.

Nor is it necessary that government, federal or regional, do all the things that government now does. A government's function is to exercise leadership, enforce standards, allocate funds, protect common purposes. The hypothesis is worth exploring that it might perform these functions better if it farmed out some of its direct service operations. If it allows insurance companies or the Blue Cross to operate without the daily assistance of government functionaries, it is not clear why recipients of Social Security checks must deal directly with the government, except as a court of last resort. If it subsidizes from a distance the building of new-model planes by private firms to support the international position of American civil aviation, it is not plain why it must be so directly involved in the management of cultural programs or educational assistance projects overseas. In between the so-called "public" and "private" sectors a large new "third sector," composed of semiautonomous public corporations and private nonprofit agencies heavily supported by government, has come into being over the last two decades. Government already relies on this sector heavily. It could rely on it more. Public services might acquire qualities of simplicity and intimacy which they now lack, and the pressure on officials in Washington and other centers of government would be proportionately reduced.

Here, and in a score of other ways, an enlightened politics could seek ways to decentralize and debureaucratize the government, and to create a middle ground on which citizens, though retaining their private status, could participate in the public business. Needless to say, this will not be easy to accomplish. It will require an ability to think in unhabitual ways about the relation of the citizen to the government, and it will meet the resistance of old structures. Bureaucrats will have to be less jealous of their jurisdictions, and the Congress will have to be willing to explore new means of supervision over the spending of public funds. The operative problem is to find a way to combine accountability for the expenditure of these funds with freedom and room to experiment for the recipient agencies.

If all this seems difficult, it can only be said that it is not likely to be nearly as difficult as bringing the American government, as it is presently constituted and as it presently conceives its functions, to a level of good performance. And to those who will say that Congress will not and should not change its traditional forms of control, it can be said that a body that has shown a spirit of liberality and genial trust toward the CIA and the Defense Department in their use of tax dollars ought to be able to show at least a little of that spirit with respect to efforts to reduce the size of the government and to increase the opportunities of citizens to participate in public affairs if they wish. The trick of supporting nongovernmental and semigovernmental organizations carrying on activities in the public interest while still leaving them autonomy has been performed in other countries. It can be performed in the United States. In fact, it has. What remains is to turn this trick into a sober, self-conscious policy.

The great obstacles, in the end, are two things: human habits and fears, intellectual and emotional, and the currently absurd allocation of our national energies, a state of affairs for which our foreign and defense policies are largely responsible. We move in a vicious circle. The government has remained insufficiently responsive to the vast national movement for change in these policies because it is rigid, vast, remote. And it is rigid, vast and remote, in large part, because it is so heavily committed, by doctrine and by the pressure of ingrown interests, to these policies.

We have not yet learned to measure the costs of foreign policy by an appropriate standard. We invoke something called "the national interest," and mean by it essentially the taking of precautions that will keep possible adversaries at a disadvantage. And since there is no limit to the damage they might want to do us, and no limit, in abstract theory, to their possible capacity at some time or other to do what they might imaginably want, there is no limit to the precautions which, in this view of the world, it is necessary and reasonable to take. And so, to ward off possible nightmares in the future, we have followed policies that involve us in nightmares in the present.

The costs of this manner of thinking are not to be figured in the national budget alone, immense though they are. They include the excessive centralization of government and the economy, the removal of major domains of national policy from close inspection by the electorate, and the neglect of problems at home and abroad more immediately and profoundly threatening to the national security. None of these is the inexorable consequence of our social system. All are the consequences of policies that overorganize and overextend it for the business of war. These policies are anachronistic, and though it is said they are justified by requirements of international security, they almost certainly raise the level of our own and other nations' insecurity. Admittedly, it is romantic to suppose that peace will break out at once if only the United States changes its ways. But a realistic assessment of the dangers that actually exist in the world—the nonmilitary as well as military dangers—suggests that we have been making unbalanced and self-destructive investments of our resources.

Indeed, the largest cost of these policies, apart from the blood that has been spilled unnecessarily, is their creation of a psychological environment that systematically undermines the authority of the government itself. They put the government at a distance from the citizens. They make it seem larger than life, harder to reach, more imperious and inhuman. As no less a philosopher than Spinoza observed, no one should expect that a government can act in accordance with the moral code appropriate to the conduct of individuals. Its problems are different. This is elementary realism about government. But a militarized foreign policy involves a government, day by day, in actions, and in defenses of these actions, that separate it too sharply from the moral sentiments of too many of those it governs. It leaves them with only two alternatives: to distrust the government, to reject its idea of law in the name of their idea of morality, or else to accept what the government does and to say that it is superior to morality. Neither of these alternatives is a possible basis for the government of a democracy.

It is half-baked realism not to realize that there are limits to the capacity of most citizens to accept the actions of the State on the grounds of reasons of State. When these limits are exceeded, or when citizens, in loyalty to the State, relax their standards, there are consequences. The moral authority of the government either declines or becomes something occult. That is the cost which the long drift of our foreign policy has begun to exact from us.

But the trauma of Vietnam has begun to break the spell. There never was a more propitious moment, if we are prepared to take advantage of it, to move the military, and the realists who are so much less than realistic, away from the center of foreign policy. If these groups recede in influence, if new men, new ideas and a saner set of priorities take over, there may be a chance to make the government work.

For this, however, something else will be needed—not a political program, but political perspective, a reasonable sense of human possibility. The government may be decrepit, disjointed and myth-ridden, but even after we have finished reforming it, it will still be an institution created by an animal whose balance with its environment is always precarious.

According to Pascal, "The most unreasonable things in the world become most reasonable because of the unruliness of men." Government is a product of unruly men, trying to control themselves while they govern other unruly men. As a consequence, if they behave in peculiar ways, and surround themselves with astonishing rules, and produce decisions that have the clarity of *Finnegans Wake* read in a thunderstorm, one shouldn't be surprised. Their confusion is the world's confusion, and there may even be purposes, sometimes good purposes, that are being served. One chooses to work inside a government, believing that some good may come from doing so, and one finds, after a while, that a certain rationality shines through. If you begin by doing what the Romans do because you are in Rome, you end by discovering that there is some charm, some intelligibility, even some inevitability, in what they do. Well, up to a point.

Author's Note

During the first months of my work on this book, the Aspen Institute for Humanistic Studies provided me with an ideal setting in which to put things in perspective. I am very grateful to the Directors of the Institute for the support and help they gave me as a "Scholar-in-Residence."

At various stages I have had the secretarial assistance of Karin Shillington, Helen Lipovsky, Ellen Stuttle and Josephine Novak. I thank them for their conscientiousness, their cheerfulness and their encouragement.

Evan Thomas has been a friend and stern critic of the manuscript, and Cass Canfield a sympathetic and patient editor. As for my wife, she knows the trouble she caused me.

I have respected the anonymity which President Johnson's assistants guarded, and have not named names when my story involves these gentlemen or others with whom I spoke in confidence.

C. F.

ABOUT THE AUTHOR

Charles Frankel has for many years been a member of the Philosophy Department at Columbia, where he has specialized in political philosophy, and has also taught in the School of Social Work and the School of International Affairs. He has been involved in a wide range of educational, public and international activities. Between 1965 and the end of 1967 he was the Assistant Secretary of State for Educational and Cultural Affairs.

An editor at large of *Saturday Review*, Mr. Frankel has also written for *Harper's Magazine*, *The New Yorker*, the *New York Times Magazine* and in many professional journals. His books include *The Case for Modern Man*, *The Democratic Prospect*, *The Love of Anxiety*, *Education and the Barricades* and *High on Foggy Bottom*.